MANUAL OF ZEN BUDDHISM

DAISETZ TEITARO SUZUKI, D.Litt

Late Professor of Buddhist Philosophy in the Otani University, Kyoto

Edited by

CHRISTMAS HUMPHREYS

Late President of the Buddhist Society, London

RIDER

LONDON MELBOURNE AUCKLAND JOHANNESBURG

First published 1950

Reissued as a Rider Pocket Edition 1983
Reprinted 1986
Rider & Company, an imprint of Century Hutchinson Limited,
Brookmount House, 62–65 Chandos Place, Covent Garden,
London WC2N 4NW

Century Hutchinson Publishing Group (Australia) Pty Ltd
16–22 Church Street, Hawthorn, Melbourne, Victoria 3122

Century Hutchinson Group (NZ) Ltd
32–34 View Road, PO Box 40–086, Glenfield, Auckland 10

Century Hutchinson Group (SA) Pty Ltd
PO Box 337, Bergvlei 2012, South Africa

British Library Cataloguing in Publication Data

Suzuki, Daisetz Teitaro
Manual of Zen Buddhism
1. Zen Buddhism
I. Title
294.3′927 BQ 9265.4

Printed and bound in Great Britain by
The Guernsey Press Co. Ltd,
Guernsey, Channel Islands

ISBN 0 09 152341 9

CONTENTS

Editor's Foreword 9
Editor's Note 11
Author's Preface 11

I GATHAS AND PRAYERS 13–20

1. On Opening the Sutra 13
2. Confession 13
3. The Threefold Refuge 14
4. The Four Great Vows 14
5. The Worshipping of the Sarira 14
6. The Teaching of the Seven Buddhas 15
7. The Gatha of Impermanence 15
8. The Yemmei Kwannon Ten-Clause Sutra 16
9. Prayer on the Occasion of Feeding the Hungry Ghosts 16
10. General Prayer 19
11. Prayer of the Bell 20

II THE DHARANIS 21–25

1. Dharani of Removing Disasters 21
2. Dharani of the Great Compassionate One 22
3. Dharani of the Victorious Buddha-Crown 23

III THE SUTRAS 26–72

1. The Prajnaparamita-hridaya-sutra, or Shingyo (complete) 26
2. The Kwannongyo, or "Samantamukha Parivarta" (complete) 30
3. The Kongokyo, or Vajracchedika (the first half and extracts from the second half) 38
4. The Lankavatara Sutra, or Ryogakyo (extracts) 50
5. The Ryogonkyo, or Surangama Sutra (résumé) 64

IV FROM THE CHINESE ZEN MASTERS 73–144

1. Bodhidharma on the Twofold Entrance to the Tao 73
2. The Third Patriarch on "Believing in Mind" 76
3. From Hui-neng's Tan-ching 82
4. Yoka Daishi's "Song of Enlightenment" 89
5. Baso (Ma-tsu) and Sekito (Shih-tou) 104
6. Obaku's (Huang-po) Sermon from "Treatise on the Essentials of the Transmission of Mind" 112
7. Gensha on the Three Invalids (from the *Hekiganshu* or *Pi-yen Chi*) 120
8. The Ten Oxherding Pictures, I 127
The Ten Oxherding Pictures, II 135

V FROM THE JAPANESE ZEN MASTERS 145–152

1. Daio Kokushi on Zen 145
2. Daio Kokushi's Admonition 146
3. Daito Kokushi's Admonition and Last Poem 147
4. Kwanzan Kokushi's Admonition 149
5. Muso Kokushi's Admonition 150
6. Hakuin's "Song of Meditation" 151

VI THE BUDDHIST STATUES AND PICTURES IN A ZEN MONASTERY 153–186

Buddhas, 153; Bodhisattvas, 161; Arhats, 168; Protecting Gods, 172; Historical Figures, 182

Index 187

LIST OF PLATES

Kwannon, by Seisetsu Seki

Bodhidharma, a Chinese Stone Rubbing

The Ten Oxherding Pictures, by Shubun, I

The Ten Oxherding Pictures, II

The Ten Oxherding Pictures, III

The Ten Oxherding Pictures, IV

The Ten Oxherding Pictures, V

The Ten Oxherding Pictures, VI

The Ten Oxherding Pictures, VII

The Ten Oxherding Pictures, VIII

The Ten Oxherding Pictures, IX

The Ten Oxherding Pictures, X

Daito Kokushi, by Hakuin Zenji

Hakuin Zenji

Bhadrapala, by Soyen

Kanzan (Han-shan) and Jittoku (Shi-te), by Kaihoku Yusho

LIST OF ILLUSTRATIONS

The Ten Oxherding Pictures, II, by an unknown master 135–144
Sakyamuni 156
Buddha with His Attendants 157
Buddha's Birth 158
Buddha's Entrance into Nirvana 159
Bhaishajyaguru 160
Manjusri 163
Samantabhadra 164
Avalokitesvara 165
Maitreya 166
Kshitigarbha 167
The Sixteen Arhats 169–171
The Two Door-keeping Gods 175
The Four Guardian Gods 176
Benzaiten (Sarasvati) 177
Sambokojin 178
Skandadeva (Idaten) 179
Ucchushma (Ususamaten) 180
Mahakala (Daikokuten) 181
Daruma (Bodhidharma), Founder of Zen 184
Shotoku Taishi 185
Fudaishi 186

EDITOR'S FOREWORD

Daisetz Teitaro Suzuki, D. Litt., Professor of Buddhist Philosophy in the Otani University, Kyoto, was born in 1870 and died in 1966. He was probably the greatest living authority on Buddhist philosophy during his life time, and was certainly the greatest authority on Zen Buddhism. His major works in English on the subject of Buddhism numbered a dozen or more and of his works in Japanese, as yet unknown in the West, there are eighteen or more. He was, moreover, as a chronological bibliography of books on Zen in English clearly shows, the pioneer of the subject outside Japan, for except for Kaiten Nukariya's *Religion of the Samurai* (Luzac and Co., 1913) nothing was known of Zen as a living experience, save to *The Eastern Buddhist* (1921-1939), until the publication of *Essays in Zen Buddhism (First Series)* in 1927.

Dr Suzuki writes with authority. Not only had he studied original works in Sanskrit, Pali, Chinese and Japanese, but he had an up-to-date knowledge of Western thought in German and French as well as in English (which he wrote and spoke so fluently). He was, moreover, more than a scholar; he was a Buddhist. Though not a priest of any Buddhist sect, he was honoured in every temple in Japan, for his knowledge of spiritual things, as all who have sat at his feet bear witness, was direct and profound. When he spoke of the higher stages of consciousness he spoke as a man who dwelt therein, and the impression he made on those who entered the fringes of his mind was that of a man who looked for the intellectual symbols wherewith to describe a state of awareness which lies indeed 'beyond the intellect'.

To those unfit to sit at the feet of the Master his writings must be a substitute. All these, however, were out of print in England by 1940, and all remaining stocks in Japan were destroyed in the fire which consumed three-quarters of Tokyo in 1945. When, therefore, I reached Japan in 1946, I arranged with the author for the Buddhist Society, London – my wife and I as its nominees – to begin publication of his

Collected Works, reprinting the old favourites, and printing as fast as possible translations of the many new works which the Professor, self-immured in his house in Kyoto, had written during the war.

This undertaking, however, was beyond the powers of the Buddhist Society, and we therefore secured the assistance of Rider and Co. who, backed by the resources of the House of Hutchinson, were able to honour the needs of such a considerable task.

Of Zen itself I need say nothing here, but the increasing sale of books on the subject proves that the interest of the West is still rising rapidly. Zen, however, is a subject extremely easy to misunderstand, and it is therefore important that the words of a genuine expert should come readily to hand.

Christmas Humphreys
Late President of the Buddhist Society, London

EDITOR'S NOTE

All references to the Author's *Essays in Zen Buddhism, Series One and Two,* and to his *Introduction to Zen Buddhism,* are to the second edition of these works, published in "The Complete Works of D. T. Suzuki."

PREFACE TO FIRST EDITION

In my *Introduction to Zen Buddhism* (published 1934), an outline of Zen teaching is sketched, and in *The Training of the Zen Monk* (1934) a description of the Meditation Hall and its life is given. To complete a triptych the present *Manual* has been compiled. The object is to inform the reader of the various literary materials relating to the monastery life. Foreign students often express their desire to know about what the Zen monk reads before the Buddha in his daily service, where his thoughts move in his leisure hours, and what objects of worship he has in the different quarters of his institution. This work will partly, it is hoped, satisfy their desire. Those who find my *Essays* too bulky or too elaborate may prefer these smaller works on Zen.

Kyoto
August 1935

DAISETZ TEITARO SUZUKI

I. GATHAS AND PRAYERS

Gatha is a Sanskrit term meaning "verse" or "hymn". In Buddhist literature it is used to designate the versified portion of the sutras. Chinese scholars have adopted this word for their versified compositions, which are known as *chieh*, an abbreviation of *chieh-t'o*, or as *chieh-sang*, which is the combination of the Sanskrit and the Chinese. The gathas collected here are not exclusively those of the Zen sect; some belong to general Buddhism.

GATHAS AND PRAYERS

I

On Opening the Sutra

The Dharma incomparably profound and exquisite
Is rarely met with, even in hundreds of thousands of
 millions of kalpas;
We are now permitted to see it, to listen to it, to
 accept and hold it;
May we truly understand the meaning of the
 Tathagata's words!

II

Confession

All the evil karma ever committed by me since of old,
On account of greed, anger, and folly, which have
 no beginning,
Born of my body, mouth, and thought—
I now make full open confession of it.

III

THE THREEFOLD REFUGE

I take refuge in the Buddha;
I take refuge in the Dharma;
I take refuge in the Sangha.
I take refuge in the Buddha, the incomparably honoured one;
I take refuge in the Dharma, honourable for its purity;
I take refuge in the Sangha, honourable for its harmonious life.
I have finished taking refuge in the Buddha;
I have finished taking refuge in the Dharma;
I have finished taking refuge in the Sangha.

IV

THE FOUR GREAT VOWS[1]

However innumerable beings are, I vow to save them;
However inexhaustible the passions are, I vow to extinguish them;
However immeasurable the Dharmas are, I vow to master them;
However incomparable the Buddha-truth is, I vow to attain it.

V

THE WORSHIPPING OF THE SARIRA

We prostrate ourselves in all humbleness before the holy Sarira representing the body of Sakyamuni, the

[1] These vows are recited after every service.

Tathagata, who is perfectly endowed with all the virtues, who has the Dharmakaya as the ground of his being, and Dharmadhatu as the stupa dedicated to him. To him we pay our respect with due deference. Manifesting himself in a bodily form for our sakes, the Buddha enters into us and makes us enter into him. His power being added to us, we attain Enlightenment; and [again] dependent on the Buddha's miraculous power, all beings are benefited, become desirous for Enlightenment, discipline themselves in the life of the Bodhisattva, and equally enter into perfect quietude where prevails infinite wisdom of absolute identity. We now prostrate ourselves before him.

VI

The Teaching of the Seven Buddhas

Not to commit evils,
But to do all that is good,
And to keep one's thought pure—
This is the teaching of all the Buddhas.

VII

The Gatha of Impermanence[1]

All composite things are impermanent,
They are subject to birth and death;
Put an end to birth and death,
And there is a blissful tranquillity.

[1] For the sake of the second half of this gatha the Buddha is said to have been willing to sacrifice his own life. For this reason this is also known as the "gatha of sacrifice".

VIII

THE YEMMEI KWANNON TEN-CLAUSE SUTRA[1]

[Adoration to] Kwanzeon!
Adoration to the Buddha!
To the Buddha we are related
In terms of cause and effect.
Depending on the Buddha, the Dharma, and the Sangha,
[Nirvana is possible which is] eternal, ever-blessed, autonomous, and free from defilements.
Every morning our thoughts are on Kwanzeon,
Every evening our thoughts are on Kwanzeon.
Every thought issues from the Mind,
Every thought is not separated from the Mind.

IX

PRAYER ON THE OCCASION OF FEEDING THE HUNGRY GHOSTS

If one wishes to know all the Buddhas of the past, present, and future, one should contemplate the nature of this Dharmadhatu essentially as the creation of Absolute Mind.

Adoration to the Buddhas in the ten quarters;

Adoration to the Dharma pervading the ten quarters;

Adoration to the Sangha in the ten quarters;

Adoration to Sakyamuni the Buddha who is our Master;

Adoration to Kwanzeon the Bodhisattva, who is the great compassionate and pitying one, ready to save beings from afflictions;

Adoration to Ananda the Arhat who is the expounder of the Teaching.

[1] *Yemmei* means "prolonging life"; when one daily recites this short document in ten clauses relating to Kwannon, one's health is assured for doing good not only for oneself but for the whole world.

Namu sabo totogyato boryakite, yen!
Sammola sammola, un!
Namu suryoboya totogyatoya tojito, yen!
Suryo suryo boya suryo boya suryo, somoko!
Namu samanda motonan, ban![1]
Adoration to Hoshin[2] the Tathagata;
Adoration to Taho[3] the Tathagata;
Adoration to Myoshishin[4] the Tathagata;
Adoration to Kohashin[5] the Tathagata;
Adoration to Rifui[6] the Tathagata;
Adoration to Kanroo[7] the Tathagata;
Adoration to Omito[8] the Tathagata.
Namu omitoboya totogyatoya,
Toniyato,
Omiritsubomi,
Omirito,
Shitabomi,
Omirito bigyaratei,
Omirito bigyarato gyamini,
Gyagyano shitogyari,

[1] It is difficult to tell how this dharani came to be inserted here. As most dharanis are, it is devoid of sense from the human point of view; but it may not be necessarily so to the hungry ghosts, for whom the prayer is offered. Can this be restored to the original Sanskrit as follows?

Namah sarva-tathagatavalokite! Om!
Sambala, sambala! hum!
Namah surupaya tathagataya!
Tadyatha,
Om, suru[paya], surupaya, surupaya, suru[paya], svaha!
Namah samantabuddhanam, vam!

"Be adored! O all the Tathagatas who are regarded [as our protectors]; Om! Provision, provision! Hum! Adored be the Tathagata Beautifully-Formed! Namely: Om! To the Beautifully-formed One! To the Beautifully-formed One! To the Beautifully-formed One! Hail! Adored be all the Buddhas! Vam!"

[2] "Jewel-excelled (*ratnaketu*).
[3] "Abundant-in-Jewel" (*prabhutaratna*).
[4] "Fine-form-body" (*surupakaya*).
[5] "Broad-wide-body" (*vipulakaya*).
[6] "Freed-from-fear" (*abhayankara*).
[7] "Nectar-king" (*amritaraja*).
[8] "Amida" (*amitabha*).

Somoko.[1]

By the supernatural power of this Dharani the food and drink is purified, and this we offer to the spiritual beings as numerous as the sands of the Ganga. We pray that they shall all be fully satisfied and abandon their greed; that they shall all leave their abodes of darkness and be born in the blissful paths of existence; and further that taking refuge in the Triple Treasure they shall awaken the desire for supreme enlightenment and finally come to the realization of it. The merit they thus attain is inexhaustible and will continue on to the end of time, making all beings equally share in this Dharma-food.

O you hosts of spiritual beings, we make this offering of food to you all, which we pray will fill the ten quarters and that all beings of your kind will partake of it.

By the practice of this meritorious deed we pray that we repay what we owe to our parents, who have done all they could for our sakes. May those who are still alive continue to enjoy their happy and prosperous lives for ever, while those who are no more with us be released from suffering and born in the land of bliss.

We pray that all sentient beings in the triple world who are recipients of the fourfold benefaction, together with those beings suffering in the three evil paths of existence and tormented with the eight kinds of calamities, may repent of all their sins and be cleansed of all their sores, so that they may all be released from the cycle of transmigration and be born in the land of purity.

We pray to all the Buddhas, all the Bodhisattva-Mahasattvas in the ten quarters, of the past, present, and future, and to Mahaprajna-paramita, that by virtue of this merit universally prevailing, not only we but all beings shall equally attain Buddhahood.

[1] Namo 'mitabhaya tathagataya! Tadyatha, amritodbhave, amritasiddhe, (?)-bhave, amritavikrante, amrita-vikranta-gamine, gaganakirtikare! Svaha!

"Adored be the Tathagata of Infinite Light! Namely: O Nectar-raising one! O Nectar-perfecting one! [O Nectar-] producing one! O One who makes nectar pervade! O One who makes nectar universally pervade! O One who makes nectar known as widely as space! Hail!"

X

GENERAL PRAYER[1]

By the Bhikshus all present here
The mystic formula of Surangama has been recited as above,
Which is now dedicated to all the Nagas and Devas who are protectors of the Dharma,
And also to all the holy assemblies of the spiritual beings who are guardians of this monastery and surrounding district.
May all beings in the three evil paths of existence variously suffering the eight kinds of disasters be thereby released from the afflictions!
May all beings in the triple world who are recipients of the fourfold benefaction thereby participate in the merit!
May the state continue in peaceful prosperity with all its warlike activities stopped!
May the wind blow in time, the rain fall seasonably, and the people live happily!
May the entire congregation sharing in the exercise cherish the higher aspirations
To go beyond the ten stages with a leap, and this without much difficulty!
May this monastery keep on its quiet life, free from disturbances.
And the patrons and devotees grow not only in faith but in wisdom and bliss!
[We pray this to] all the Buddhas and Bodhisattva-
Mahasattvas in the ten quarters, of the past, present, and future, and to Mahaprajna-paramita!

[1] This is read, as can be inferred from the text, after the recitation of the Surangama dharani.

XI

Prayer of the Bell

Would that the sound of the bell might go beyond our earth,
And be heard even by all the denizens of the darkness outside the Iron Mountains (*cakravala*)!
Would that, their organ of hearing becoming pure, beings might attain perfect interfusion [of all the senses],
So that every one of them might come finally to the realization of supreme enlightenment![1]

[1] It is customary in the Zen monastery to recite the *Kwannongyo* while striking the big bell, which is done three times a day. The present gatha is recited when the striking is finished. As will be seen below, from Kwannon issues a sound which is heard by those who sincerely believe in his power of releasing them from every form of disaster. Each sound emitted by the bell is the voice of Kwannon calling on us to purify our sense of hearing, whereby a spiritual experience called "interfusion" will finally take place in us. See under the *Ryogonkyo* and the *Kwannongyo* below.

II. THE DHARANIS

Properly speaking, the dharani has no legitimate place in Zen. That it has nevertheless crept into its daily service is due to the general characteristics of Chinese Buddhism of the Sung dynasty, when the Japanese Zen masters visited China and imported it as they found it then, together with the Shingon elements of Chinese Zen. In China the Shingon did not thrive very long but left its traces in Zen.

Dharani, the root of which is *dhr*, "to hold" or "to convey", is ordinarily translated by the Chinese *tsung-ch'ih*, "general holder", or *neng-ch'ih*, "that which holds". A dharani is considered as holding magical power in it or bearing deep meaning. When it is pronounced, whatever evil spirits there are ready to interfere with the spiritual effect of a ritual, are kept away from it.

In the following pages the three most frequently read dharanis are given. When translated they convey no intelligent signification. They mostly consist of invocations and exclamations. The invocation is an appeal to the higher powers, and the exclamation is to frighten away the evil spirits. That the practical result of these utterances is not to be judged objectively goes without saying.

THE DHARANIS

I

Dharani of Removing Disasters

Adoration to all the Buddhas!
Adoration to the Teaching that knows no obstructions!
Thus:
Om! Khya khya khyahi khyahi (speak, speak)!
Hum hum!
Jvala jvala prajvala prajvala (blaze, blaze)!
Tistha tistha (up, up)!

Stri stri (?)!
Sphata (burst, burst)!
One who is quiescent!
To the glorious one, hail!

II

Dharani of the Great Compassionate One

Adoration to the Triple Treasure!

Adoration to Avalokitesvara the Bodhisattva-Mahasattva who is the great compassionate one!

Om, to the one who performs a leap beyond all fears!

Having adored him, may I enter into the heart of the blue-necked one known as the noble adorable Avalokitesvara! It means the completing of all meaning, it is pure, it is that which makes all beings victorious and cleanses the path of existence.

Thus:
Om, the seer, the world-transcending one!
O Hari the Mahabodhisattva!
All, all!
Defilement, defilement!
The earth, the earth!
It is the heart.
Do, do the work!
Hold fast, hold fast!
O great victor!
Hold on, hold on!
I hold on.
To Indra the creator!
Move, move, my defilement-free seal!
Come, come!
Hear, hear!
A joy springs up in me!
Speak, speak! Directing!

Hulu, hulu, mala, hulu, hulu, hile!
Sara, sara! siri, siri! suru, suru!
Be awakened, be awakened!
Have awakened, have awakened!
O merciful one, blue-necked one!
Of daring ones, to the joyous, hail!
To the successful one, hail!
To the great successful one, hail!
To the one who has attained mastery in the discipline, hail!
To the blue-necked one, hail!
To the boar-faced one, hail!
To the one with a lion's head and face, hail!
To the one who holds a weapon in his hand, hail!
To the one who holds a wheel in his hand, hail!
To the one who holds a lotus in his hand, hail!
To the blue-necked far-causing one, hail!
To the beneficient one referred to in this Dharani beginning with "Namah," hail!
Adoration to the Triple Treasure!
Adoration to Avalokitesvara!
Hail!
May these [prayers] be successful!
To this magical formula, hail!

III

Dharani of the Victorious Buddha-Crown

Adoration to the Blessed One who is the most excellent one in the triple world!

Adoration to the Enlightened One, to the Blessed One!
Namely:
Om! Cleanse [us], cleanse [us]! O one who is always

impartial! One who, being in possession of all-pervading, all-illuminating light, is pure in his self-nature, cleansed of the darkness of the five paths of existence!

Baptize us, O Sugata, with an immortal baptism which consists of the best words, of the great true phrases!

Remove disasters, remove disasters, O one who holds an eternal life!

Cleanse us, cleanse us, O one who is as pure as the sky!

O one who is as pure as the victorious Buddha-crown!

O one who is inflamed with a thousand rays of light!

O all the Tathagatas who look over [the entire world]!

O one who is perfect in the Six Paramitas!

O one who holds the great seal empowered with the spiritual power which emanates from the heart of every Tathagata!

O one whose body is as hard and pure as Vajra!

O one who is thoroughly pure, cleansed of all impediments, all fears, and all the evil paths!

Turn us away [from evils] O one who enjoys a purified life!

O one who empowers us with [the power of] the original covenant! O jewel, jewel, the great jewel! O Suchness which is reality-limit and absolute purity!

O one who is pure in his evolved enlightenment!

Be victorious, be victorious, be ever victorious, be ever victorious!

Bear in mind, bear in mind!

O one who is pure being empowered by all Buddhas!

O Vajragarbha who holds the Vajra! Let my body be like Vajra! Let those of all beings too be like Vajra!

O one who is in possession of an absolutely pure body! O one who is absolutely pure from all the paths of existence! And let me be consoled by all the Tathagatas!

O one who is empowered with the consoling power of all the Tathagatas!

Be enlightened, be enlightened, be ever enlightened, be ever enlightened!

Have them enlightened, have them enlightened, have them ever enlightened, have them ever enlightened!

O one who is most pure in a most thoroughgoing way!

O one who holds a great seal empowered with the spiritual power which emanates from the heart of every Tathagata!

Hail!

III. THE SUTRAS

The sutras most read in Zen are the *Shingyo* (*Prajnaparamitahridaya*), the *Kwannongyo* (*Samantamukha-parivarta*), and the *Kongokyo* (*Vajracchedika*). The *Shingyo* being the shortest is read on almost all occasions. The *Ryoga* (*Lankavatara*) is historically significant, but being difficult to understand is very little studied nowadays by followers of Zen. For further information see the author's works on the sutra. The *Ryogon* (*Suramgama*) is not so neglected as the *Ryoga*. It is full of deep thoughts, and was studied very much more in China than in Japan. There are some more sutras of the Mahayana school with which Zen students will do well to become better acquainted, for example, the *Kongosammaikyo* (*Vajrasamadhi*), the *Yengakukyo* (Sutra of Perfect Enlightenment), the *Yuimakyo* (*Vimalakirti-sutra*), and *the Hannyakyo* (*Prajnaparamita*). None of them have been translated into English, except the *Yuima* which is difficult to obtain now.

THE SUTRAS

I

English Translation Of The Shingyo

When[1] the Bodhisattva Avalokitesvara was engaged in the practice of the deep Prajnaparamita, he perceived that there are the five Skandhas;[2] and these he saw in their self-nature to be empty.[3]

"O Sariputra, form is here emptiness,[4] emptiness is form; form is no other than emptiness, emptiness is no other than form; that which is form is emptiness, that which is emptiness is form. The same can be said of sensation, thought, confection, and consciousness.

"O Sariputra, all things here are characterized with emptiness: they are not born, they are not annihilated; they are not tainted, they are not immaculate; they do not increase, they do not decrease. Therefore, O Sariputra, in emptiness there is no form, no sensation, no thought, no confection, no consciousness; no eye,[5] ear, nose, tongue, body, mind; no form,[6] sound, colour, taste, touch, objects; no Dhatu of vision,[7] till we come to[8] no Dhatu of consciousness; there is no knowledge, no ignorance,[9] till we come to there is no old age and death, no extinction of old age and death; there is no suffering,[10] no accumulation, no annihilation, no path; there is no knowledge, no attainment, [and] no realization,* because there is no attainment. In the mind of the Bodhisattva who dwells depending on the Pranjaparamita there are no obstacles;† and, going beyond the perverted views, he reaches final Nirvana. All the Buddhas of the past, present, and future, depending on the Pranjaparamita, attain to the highest perfect enlightenment.

"Therefore, one ought to know that the Prajnaparamita is the great Mantram, the Mantram of great wisdom, the highest Mantram, the peerless Mantram, which is capable of allaying all pain; it is truth because it is not falsehood: this is the Mantram proclaimed in the *Prajnaparamita*. It runs: '*Gate, gate, paragate, parasamgate, bodhi, svaha*!' (O Bodhi, gone, gone, gone to the other shore, landed at the other shore, Svaha!)"

NOTES

1. There are two texts with the title of *The Hridaya*: the one is known as the Shorter and the other the Larger. The one printed above is the shorter sutra in general use in Japan and China.

The opening passage in the larger text in Sanskrit and Tibetan, which is missing in the shorter one, is as follows: [The Tibetan has this additional passage: "Adoration to the Prajnaparamita, which is beyond words, thought, and praise, whose

* *Nabhisamayah* is missing in the Chinese translations as well as in the Horyuji MS.

† For *varana* all the Chinese have "obstacle", and this is in full accord with the teaching of the *Prajnaparamita*. Max Muller's rendering, "envelop", is not good.

self-nature is, like unto space, neither created nor destroyed, which is a state of wisdom and morality evident to our inner consciousness, and which is the mother of all Excellent Ones of the past, present, and future".] "Thus I heard. At one time the World-honoured One dwelt at Rajagriha, on the Mount of Vulture, together with a large number of Bhikshus and a large number of Bodhisattvas. At that time the World-honoured One was absorbed in a Samadhi (Meditation) known as Deep Enlightenment. And at the same moment the Great Bodhisattva Aryavalokitesvara was practising himself in the deep Prajnaparamita."

The concluding passage, which is also missing in the shorter text, runs as follows:

"O Sariputra, thus should the Bodhisattva practise himself in the deep Prajnaparamita. At that moment, the World-honoured One rose from the Samadhi and gave approval to the Great Bodhisattva Aryavalokitesvara, saying: Well done, well done, noble son! so it is! so should the practice of the deep Prajnaparamita be carried on. As it has been preached by you, it is applauded by Tathagatas and Arhats. Thus spoke the World-honoured One with joyful heart. The venerable Sariputra and the Great Bodhisattva Aryavalokitesvara together with the whole assemblage, and the world of Gods, Men, Asuras, and Gandharvas, all praised the speech of the World-honoured One."

2. From the modern scientific point of view, the conception of Skandha seems to be too vague and indefinite. But we must remember that the Buddhist principle of analysis is not derived from mere scientific interest; it aims at saving us from the idea of an ultimate individual reality which is imagined to exist as such for all the time to come. For when this idea is adhered to as final, the error of attachment is committed, and it is this attachment that forever enslaves us to the tyranny of external things. The five Skandhas ("aggregates" or "elements") are form (*rupam*), sensation or sense-perception (*vedana*), thought (*samjna*), confection or conformation (*samskara*), and consciousness (*vijnana*). The first Skandha is the material world or the materiality of things, while the remaining four Skandhas belong to the mind. *Vedana* is what we get through our senses; *samjna* corresponds to thought in its broadest sense, or that which mind elaborates; *samskara* is a very difficult term and there is no exact English equivalent; it means something that gives form, formative principle; *vijnana* is consciousness or mentation.

There are six forms of mentation, distinguishable as seeing, hearing, smelling, tasting, touching, and thinking.

3. Hsuan-chuang's translation has this added: "He was delivered from all suffering and misery."

4. "Empty" (*sunya*) or "emptiness" (*sunyata*) is one of the most important notions in Mahayana philosophy and at the same time the most puzzling for non-Buddhist readers to comprehend. Emptiness does not mean "relativity", or "phenomenality", or "nothingness", but rather means the Absolute, or something of transcendental nature, although this rendering is also misleading as we shall see later. When Buddhists declare all things to be empty, they are not advocating a nihilistic view; on the contrary an ultimate reality is hinted at, which cannot be subsumed under the categories of logic. With them, to proclaim the conditionality of things is to point to the existence of something altogether unconditioned and transcendent of all determination. Sunyata may thus often be most appropriately rendered by the Absolute. When the sutra says that the five Skandhas have the character of emptiness, or that in emptiness there is neither creation nor destruction, neither defilement nor immaculacy, etc., the sense is: no limiting qualities are to be attributed to the Absolute; while it is immanent in all concrete and particular objects, it is not in itself definable. Universal negation, therefore, in the philosophy of Prajna is an inevitable outcome.

5. No eye, no ear, etc., refer to the six senses. In Buddhist philosophy, mind (*manovijnana*) is the special sense-organ for the apprehension of *dharma*, or objects of thought.

6. No form, no sound, etc., are the six qualities of the external world, which become objects of the six senses.

7. "Dhatu of vision, etc." refer to the eighteen Dhatus or elements of existence, which include the six senses (*indriya*), the six qualities (*vishaya*), and the six consciousnesses (*vijnana*).

8. "Till we come to" (*yavat* in Sanskrit, and *nai chih* in Chinese) is quite frequently met with in Buddhist literature to avoid repetition of well-known subjects. These classifications may seem somewhat confusing and overlapping.

9. "There is no knowledge, no ignorance, etc." is the wholesale denial of the Twelvefold Chain of Causation (*pratityasamutpada*), which are ignorance (*avidya*), deed (*samskara*), consciousness (*vijnana*), name and form (*namarupa*), six sense-organs (*sadayatana*), contact (*sparsa*), sense-perception (*vedana*), desire (*trishna*), attachment (*upadana*), being (*bhava*), birth (*jati*), and old

age and death (*jaramarana*). This Chain of Twelve has been a subject of much discussion among Buddhist scholars.

10. The allusion is of course to the Fourfold Noble Truth (*satya*): 1. Life is suffering (*duhkha*); 2. Because of the accumulation (*samudaya*) of evil karma; 3. The cause of suffering can be annihilated (*nirodha*); 4. And for this there is the path (*marga*).

II

The Kwannon Sutra[1]

At that time Mujinni[2] Bosatsu rose from his seat, and, baring his right shoulder, turned, with his hands folded, towards the Buddha, and said this: World-honoured One, for what reason is Kwanzeon Bosatsu so named?

The Buddha said to Mujinni Bosatsu: Good man, when those innumerable numbers of beings—hundred-thousands of myriads of kotis of them—who are suffering all kinds of annoyances, hearing of this Kwanzeon Bosatsu, will utter his name with singleness of mind, they will instantly hear his voice and be released.

Even when people fall into a great fire, if they hold the name of Kwanzeon Bosatsu, the fire will not scorch them because of the spiritual power of this Bosatsu. When they are

[1] Generally known as *Kwannon-gyo* in Japanese and *Kuan-yin Ching* in Chinese. It forms the Twenty-fifth Chapter in Kumarajiva's translation of the *Saddharma-pundarika*, "the Lotus of the Good Law". Its Sanskrit title is *Samantamukha Parivarta*. It is one of the most popular sutras in Japan, especially among followers of the Holy Path, including Zen, Tendai, Shingon, Nichiren, etc.

The Sanskrit for *Kwannon* seems, according to some Japanese authorities, originally to have been *Avalokitasvara*, and not *Avalokitesvara*. If so, *Kwannon* is a more literal rendering than *Kwanzeon* (*Kuan-shih-yin*) or *Kwanjizai* (*Kuan-tzu-tsai*). The Bodhisattva Avalokitasvara is "the owner of *voice which is viewed* or heard". From him issues a voice which is variously heard and interpreted by all beings, and it is by this hearing that the latter are emancipated from whatever troubles they are in.

The present translation is from Kumarajiva's Chinese. In the reading of the proper names, the Japanese way of pronunciation has been retained.

[2] Bodhisattva Akshayamati in Sanskrit, that is, Bodhisattva of Inexhaustible Intelligence.

tossed up and down in the surging waves, if they pronounce his name they will get into a shallower place.

When hundred-thousands of myriads of kotis of people go out into the great ocean in order to seek such treasures as gold, silver, lapis lazuli, conch shells, cornelian, coral, amber, pearls, and other precious stones, their boats may be wrecked by black storms, and they may find themselves thrown up into the island of the Rakshasas; if among them there is even a single person who will utter the name of Kwanzeon Bosatsu all the people will be released from the disaster [which is likely to befall them at the hand] of the Rakshasas. For this reason the Bosatsu is called Kwanzeon.

When, again, a man is about to suffer an injury, if he will utter the name of Kwanzeon Bosatsu, the sword or the stick that is held [by the executioner] will be at once broken to pieces and the man be released.

When all the Yakshas and Rakshasas filling the three thousand chiliocosms come and annoy a man, they may hear him utter the name of Kwanzeon Bosatsu, and no wicked spirits will dare look at him with their evil eyes, much less inflict injuries on him.

When again a man, whether guilty or innocent, finds himself bound in chains or held with manacles, he uttering the name of Kwanzeon Bosatsu will see all these broken to pieces and be released.

When all the lands in the three thousand chiliocosms are filled with enemies, a merchant and his caravan loaded with precious treasures may travel through the dangerous passes. One of the company will say to the others: "O good men, have no fear; only with singleness of thought utter the name of Kwanzeon Bosatsu. As this Bosatsu gives us fearlessness, utter his name and you will be delivered from your enemies." Hearing this, all the company join in the recitation, saying, "Kwanzeon Bosatsu be adored!" Because of this uttering the name of the Bosatsu they will be released. O Mujinni, such is the awe-inspiring spiritual power of Kwanzeon Bosatsu Makasatsu.

When people are possessed of excessive lust, let them

always reverentially think of Kwanzeon Bosatsu and they will be freed from it. If they are possessed of excessive anger, let them always reverentially think of Kwanzeon Bosatsu, and they will be freed from it. When they are possessed of excessive folly let them always reverentially think of Kwanzeon Bosatsu, and they will be freed from it. O Mujinni, of such magnitude is his spiritual power which is full of blessings. Therefore, let all beings always think of him.

If a woman desire a male child, let her worship and make offerings to Kwanzeon Bosatsu, and she will have a male child fully endowed with bliss and wisdom. If she desire a female child, she will have one graceful in features and in possession of all the characteristics [of noble womanhood], and because of her having planted the root of merit the child will be loved and respected by all beings. O Mujinni, such is the power of Kwanzeon Bosatsu.

If all beings worship and make offerings to Kwanzeon Bosatsu, they will derive benefits unfailingly from this. Therefore, let all beings hold the name of Kwanzeon Bosatsu. O Mujinni, if there is a man who holds the names of all the Bodhisattvas equal in number to sixty-two billion times as many as the sands of the Ganga, and till the end of his life makes them offerings of food and drink, clothing and bedding and medicine, what do you think? Is not the merit accumulated by such a man very great?

Mujinni said: Very great, indeed, World-honoured One!

The Buddha said: Here is another man; if he should hold the name of Kwanzeon Bosatsu even for a while and make offerings to the Bosatsu, the merit so attained by this one is fully equal to that [of the previous one], and will not be exhausted even to the end of hundred-thousands of myriads of kotis of kalpas. Those who hold the name of Kwanzeon Bosatsu gain such immeasurable and innumerable masses of blissful merit.

Mujinni Bosatsu said to the Buddha: "World-honoured One, how does Kwanzeon Bosatsu visit this Saha world?[1]

[1] That is, *sahaloka*, world of patience.

How does he preach the Dharma to all beings? What is the extent of his skilful means?

The Buddha said to Mujinni Bosatsu: O good man, if there are beings in any country who are to be saved by his assuming a Buddha-form, Kwanzeon Bosatsu will manifest himself in the form of a Buddha and preach them the Dharma.

If beings are to be saved by his assuming a Pratyekabuddha-form, the Bosatsu will manifest himself in the form of a Pratyekabuddha and preach them the Dharma.

If beings are to be saved by his assuming a Sravaka-form, the Bosatsu will manifest himself in the form of a Sravaka and preach them the Dharma.

If beings are to be saved by his assuming a Brahma-form, the Bosatsu will manifest himself in the form of a Brahma and preach them the Dharma.

If beings are to be saved by his assuming a Sakrendra-form, the Bosatsu will manifest himself in the form of a Sakrendra and preach them the Dharma.

If beings are to be saved by his assuming an Isvara-form, the Bosatsu will manifest himself in the form of an Isvara and preach them the Dharma.

If beings are to be saved by his assuming a Mahesvara-form, he will manifest himself in the form of a Mahesvara and preach them the Dharma.

If beings are to be saved by his assuming a Chakravartin-form, the Bosatsu will manifest himself in the form of a Chakravartin and preach them the Dharma.

If beings are to be saved by his assuming a Vaisravana-form, the Bosatsu will manifest himself in the form of a Vaisravana and preach them the Dharma.

If beings are to be saved by his assuming the form of a provincial chief, the Bosatsu will manifest himself in the form of a provincial chief and preach them the Dharma.

If beings are to be saved by his assuming a householder's form, the Bosatsu will manifest himself in the form of a householder and preach them the Dharma.

If beings are to be saved by his assuming a lay-disciple's

form, the Bosatsu will manifest himself in the form of a lay-disciple and preach them the Dharma.

If beings are to be saved by his assuming a state-officer's form, the Bosatsu will manifest himself in the form of a state-officer and preach them the Dharma.

If beings are to be saved by his assuming a Brahman-form, the Bosatsu will manifest himself to them in the form of a Brahman and preach them the Dharma.

If beings are to be saved by his assuming a Bhikshu-form, or a Bhikshuni-, or an Upasaka-, or an Upasika-form, the Bosatsu will manifest himself in the form of a Bhikshu, or a Bhikshuni, or an Upasaka, or an Upasika, and preach them the Dharma.

If beings are to be saved by his assuming a female form of the family of a householder, or a lay-disciple, or a state-officer, or a Brahman, the Bosatsu will manifest himself in the form of such a female and preach them the Dharma.

If beings are to be saved by his assuming a youth- or a maiden-form, the Bosatsu will manifest himself in the form of a youth or a maiden and preach them the Dharma.

If beings are to be saved by his assuming a Deva-, Naga-, Yaksha-, Gandharva-, Asura-, Garuda-, Kinnara-, Mahoraga-, Manushya-, or Amanushya-form, the Bosatsu will manifest himself in any of these forms and preach them the Dharma.

If beings are to be saved by his assuming a Vajrapani-form, the Bosatsu will manifest himself in the form of Vajrapani and preach them the Dharma.

O Mujinni, this Kwanzeon Bosatsu performs such meritorious deeds by assuming varieties of forms, and by visiting different lands saves and releases beings. Therefore, you will make offerings with singleness of thought to Kwanzeon Bosatsu. In the midst of fears, perils, and disasters, it is he who gives us fearlessness,[1] and for this reason he is called in this Saha world the one who gives fearlessness.

Mujinni Bosatsu said to the Buddha: I wish now to make

[1] "Safety", or better "faith".

an offering to Kwanzeon Bosatsu. So saying, he took off his necklace strung with all kinds of precious gems worth hundreds of thousands of gold pieces, and presented it to Kwanzeon Bosatsu with this word: Venerable Sir, accept this necklace of precious gems as a Dharma offering.

Kwanzeon Bosatsu refused to accept it, whereupon Mujinni said to him: Venerable Sir, Pray accept this out of compassion for us all.

Then the Buddha said to Kwanzeon Bosatsu: Out of compassion for Mujinni Bosatsu and all the four classes of beings, and also for the Devas, Nagas, Yakshas, Gandharvas, Asuras, Garudas, Kinnaras, Mahoragas, Manushyas, Amanushyas and others, accept, O Kwanzeon Bosatsu, this necklace of his.

Then because of his compassion for all the four classes of beings and for Devas, Nagas, Manushyas, Amanushyas and others, Kwanzeon Bosatsu accepted the necklace, and dividing it into two parts he presented the one to Shakamunibutsu (Sakyamuni Buddha) and the other to the shrine of Tahobutsu (Prabhutaratna Buddha).

O Mujinni, Kwanzeon Bosatsu who is the possessor of such a miraculous spiritual power, visits in this wise this Saha world.

At that time Mujinni Bosatsu asked in verse, saying:

O World-honoured One who is in possession of exquisite features, I now again ask him: For what reason is the son of the Buddha called Kwanzeon?

The Honoured One in possession of exquisite features answered Mujinni in verse: Just listen to the life of Kwanzeon! He is always ready to respond to calls from all quarters. His universal vows are as deep as the ocean. For ages beyond conception, he has served myriads of Buddhas and made great vows of purity.

I will briefly tell you about them. When people hear his name and see his body and think of him in their minds not vainly, they will see every form of ill effaced in all the worlds.

If an enemy wishing to harm a man pushes him down

to a pit of great fire, let his thought dwell on the power of Kwannon and the fiery pit will be transformed into a pond.

Or if drifting in the vast ocean a man is about to be swallowed up by the Nagas, fishes, or évil beings, let his thought dwell on the power of Kwannon, and the waves will not drown him.

Or if from the top of Mount Sumeru a man is hurled down by an enemy, let his thought dwell on the power of Kwannon, and he will stay in the air like the sun.

Or if pursued by wicked persons a man falls on the Vajra mountain, let his thought dwell on the power of Kwannon, and not a hair on him will be injured.

Or if surrounded by an army of enemies a man is threatened by them, each of whom with a sword in hand is about to injure him, let his thought dwell on the power of Kwannon, and the enemies will cherish a compassionate heart.

Or if persecuted by a tyrant a man is about to end his life at the place of execution, let his thought dwell on the power of Kwannon, and the executioner's sword will at once be broken to pieces.

Or if a man should find himself imprisoned and enchained with his hands and feet manacled and fettered, let his thought dwell on the power of Kwannon, and he will be released from the shackles.

If harm is going to be done to a man by means of magic or poisonous herbs, let his thought dwell on the power of Kwannon, and the curse will revert to the people from whom it started.

Or if a man should encounter a party of Rakshasas, or Nagas exhaling poison, or evil spirits, let his thought dwell on the power of Kwannon, and no harm will ever be done to him.

If a man is surrounded by wild beasts whose sharp teeth and claws are to be dreaded, let his thought dwell on the power of Kwannon, and they will quickly run away in all directions.

If a man is attacked by venomous snakes and scorpions

breathing poisonous gas ready to scorch him, let his thought dwell on the power of Kwannon, and they will all turn away from him shrieking.

When thunder-clouds burst with flashes of lightning, causing a storm of hailstones or pouring rain in torrents, let your thought dwell on the power of Kwannon and the storm will in no time clear away.

If a calamity falls on beings and they are tortured with interminable pain, [let them resort to] Kwannon who, being endowed with the mysterious power of wisdom, will save them from all troubles in the world.

Kwannon is the possessor of miraculous powers, widely disciplined in knowledge and skilful means, and in all the lands of the ten quarters there is not a place where he does not manifest himself.

The various evil paths of existence such as hells, evil spirits, beastly creatures, etc., and the pains arising from birth, old age, disease, and death—they will all by degrees be annihilated.

[Kwannon is] the one who views the world in truth, free from defilement, with knowledge extending far, and full of love and compassion; he is to be always prayed to and always adored.

He is a pure, spotless light and, like the sun, dispels all darkness with wisdom, and also subverts the disastrous effects of wind and fire; his all-illuminating light fills the world.

His body of love he keeps under control like thunder that shakes the world; his thought of compassion resembles a great mass of cloud from which a rain of the Dharma comes down like nectar, destroying the flames of evil passions.

If a man is held at court with a case against him, or if he is intimidated at a military camp, let his thought dwell on the power of Kwannon, and all his enemies will beat retreat.

[His is] a most exquisite voice, a voice that surveys the world, the voice of Brahma, the voice of the ocean—one that excels all the voices of the world. For this reason let our thought always dwell on him.

Let us never cherish thoughts of doubt about Kwanzeon

who is thoroughly pure and holy and is really a refuge and protector in trouble, grief, death, and disaster.

He is in possession of all merits, regards all things with an eye of compassion, and like the ocean holds in himself an inestimable mass of virtues. For this reason he is to be adored.

At that time Jiji Bosatsu[1] rose from his seat, and standing before the Buddha said: World-honoured One, they are truly furnished with no small amount of merit who listen to his Chapter on Kwanzeon Bosatsu, in which his life of perfect activities is described—the life of one who, endowed with miraculous powers, manifests himself in all directions.

When the Buddha finished preaching this Chapter on the All-sided One all the people in the assembly, amounting to 84,000 in number, cherished the desire for the supreme enlightenment with which there is nothing to compare.

III

The Kongokyo or Diamond Sutra[2]

1. Thus I have heard.

At one time the Buddha stayed at Anathapindaka's Garden in the grove of Jeta in the kingdom of Sravasti; he was together with 1,250 great Bhikshus. When the meal time came the World-honoured One put on his cloak and, holding his bowl, entered the great city of Sravasti, where he begged for food. Having finished his begging from door to door, he came back to his own place, and took his meal.

[1] Dharanindhara in Sanskrit, "the supporter of the earth".

[2] *Kongokyo* in Japanese. The full title in Sanskrit is *Vajracchedika-prajna-paramita-sutra*. It belongs to the Prajna class of Mahayana literature. Those who are not accustomed to this kind of reasoning may wonder what is the ultimate signification of all these negations. The Prajna dialectic means to lead us to a higher affirmation by contradicting a simple direct statement. It differs from the Hegelian in its directness and intuitiveness.

The present English translation is from Kumarajiva's Chinese version made between 402–412 C.E.

When this was done, he put away his cloak and bowl, washed his feet, spread his seat, and sat down.

2. Then the Venerable Subhuti, who was among the assembly, rose from his seat, bared his right shoulder, set his right knee on the ground, and, respectfully folding his hands, addressed the Buddha thus:

"It is wonderful, World-honoured One, that the Tathagata thinks so much of all the Bodhisattvas and instructs them so well. World-honoured One, in case good men and good women ever raise the desire for the Supreme Enlightenment, how would they abide in it? how would they keep their thoughts under control?"

The Buddha said: "Well said, indeed, O Subhuti! As you say, the Tathagata thinks very much of all the Bodhisattvas, and so instructs them well. But now listen attentively and I will tell you. In case good men and good women raise the desire for the Supreme Enlightenment, they should thus abide in it, they should thus keep their thoughts under control."

"So be it, World-honoured One, I wish to listen to you."

3. The Buddha said to Subhuti: "All the Bodhisattva-Mahasattvas should thus keep their thoughts under control. All kinds of beings such as the egg-born, the womb-born, the moisture-born, the miraculously-born, those with form, those without form, those with consciousness, those without consciousness, those with no-consciousness, and those without no-consciousness—they are all led by me to enter Nirvana that leaves nothing behind and to attain final emancipation. Though thus beings immeasurable, innumerable, and unlimited are emancipated, there are in reality no beings that are ever emancipated. Why, Subhuti? If a Bodhisattva retains the thought of an ego, a person, a being, or a soul, he is no more a Bodhisattva.

4. "Again, Subhuti, when a Bodhisattva practises charity he should not be cherishing any idea, that is to say, he is not to cherish the idea of a form when practising charity, nor is he to cherish the idea of a sound, an odour,

a touch, or a quality.[1] Subhuti, a Bodhisattva should thus practise charity without cherishing any idea of form. Why? When a Bodhisattva practises charity without cherishing any idea of form, his merit will be beyond conception. Subhuti, what do you think? Can you have the conception of space extending eastward?"

"No, World-honoured One, I cannot."

"Subhuti, can you have the conception of space extending towards the south, or west, or north, or above, or below?"

"No, World-honoured One, I cannot."

"Subhuti, so it is with the merit of a Bodhisattva who practises charity without cherishing any idea of form; it is beyond conception. Subhuti, a Bodhisattva should cherish only that which is taught to him.

5. "Subhuti, what do you think? Is the Tathagata to be recognized after a body-form?"

"No, World-honoured One, he is not to be recognized after a body-form. Why? According to the Tathagata, a body-form is not a body-form."

The Buddha said to Subhuti, "All that has a form is an illusive existence. When it is perceived that all form is no-form, the Tathagata is recognized."

6. Subhuti said to the Buddha: "World-honoured One, if beings hear such words and statements, would they have a true faith in them?"

The Buddha said to Subhuti: "Do not talk that way. In the last five hundred years after the passing of the Tathagata, there may be beings who, having practised rules of morality and, being thus possessed of merit, happen to hear of these statements and rouse a true faith in them. Such beings, you must know, are those who have planted their root of merit not only under one, two, three, four, or five Buddhas, but already under thousands of myriads of asamkhyeyas of Buddhas have they planted their root of merit of all kinds. Those who hearing these statements rouse even one thought

[1] *Dharma*, that is, the object of *manovijnana*, thought, as form (*rupa*) is the object of the visual sense, sound that of the auditory sense, odour that of the olfactory sense, and so forth.

of pure faith, Subhuti, are all known to the Tathagata, and recognized by him as having acquired such an immeasurable amount of merit. Why? Because all these beings are free from the idea of an ego, a person, a being, or a soul; they are free from the idea of a dharma as well as from that of a no-dharma. Why? Because if they cherish in their minds the idea of a form, they are attached to an ego, a person, a being, or a soul. If they cherish the idea of a dharma, they are attached to an ego, a person, a being, or a soul. Why? If they cherish the idea of a no-dharma, they are attached to an ego, a person, a being, or a soul. Therefore, do not cherish the idea of a dharma, nor that of a no-dharma. For this reason, the Tathagata always preaches thus: 'O you Bhikshus, know that my teaching is to be likened unto a raft. Even a dharma is cast aside, much more a no-dharma.'

7. "Subhuti, what do you think? Has the Tathagata attained the supreme enlightenment? Has he something about which he would preach?"

Subhuti said: "World-honoured One, as I understand the teaching of the Buddha, there is no fixed doctrine about which the Tathagata would preach. Why? Because the doctrine he preaches is not to be adhered to, nor is it to be preached about; it is neither a dharma nor a no-dharma. How is it so? Because all wise men belong to the category known as non-doing (*asamskara*), and yet they are distinct from one another.

8. "Subhuti, what do you think? If a man should fill the three thousand chiliocosms with the seven precious treasures and give them all away for charity, would not the merit he thus obtains be great?"

Subhuti said: "Very great, indeed, World-honoured One."

"Why? Because their merit is characterized with the quality of not being a merit. Therefore, the Tathagata speaks of the merit as being great. If again there is a man who, holding even the four lines in this sutra, preaches about it to others, his merit will be superior to the one just mentioned. Because, Subhuti, all the Buddhas and their supreme enlightenment issue from this sutra. Subhuti, what is known as the teaching of the Buddha is not the teaching of the Buddha.

9. "Subhuti, what do you think? Does a Srotapanna think in this wise: 'I have obtained the fruit of Srotapatti'?"

Subhuti said: "No, World-honoured One, he does not. Why? Because while Srotapanna means 'entering the stream' there is no entering here. He is called a Srotapanna who does not enter [a world of] form, sound, odour, taste, touch, and quality.

"Subhuti, what do you think? Does a Sakridagamin think in this wise, 'I have obtained the fruit of a Sakridagamin'?"

Subhuti said: "No, World-honoured One, he does not. Why? Because while Sakridagamin means 'going-and-coming for once', there is really no going-and-coming here, and he is then called a Sakridagamin."

"Subhuti, what do you think? Does an Anagamin think in this wise: 'I have obtained the fruit of an Anagamin'?"

Subhuti said: "No, World-honoured One, he does not. Why? Because while Anagamin means 'not-coming' there is really no not-coming and therefore he is called an Anagamin."

"Subhuti, what do you think? Does an Arhat think in this wise: 'I have obtained Arhatship'?"

Subhuti said: "No, World-honoured One, he does not. Why? Because there is no dharma to be called Arhat. If, World-honoured One, an Arhat thinks in this wise: 'I have obtained Arhatship,' this means that he is attached to an ego, a person, a being, or a soul. Although the Buddha says that I am the foremost of those who have attained Arana-samadhi,[1] that I am the foremost of those Arhats who are liberated from evil desires, World-honoured One, I cherish no such thought that I have attained Arhatship. World-honoured One, [if I did,] you would not tell me: 'O Subhuti,

[1] That is, Samadhi of non-resistance. *Arana* also means a forest where the Yogin retires to practise his meditation.

you are one who enjoys the life of non-resistance.' Just because Subhuti is not at all attached to this life, he is said to be the one who enjoys the life of non-resistance."

10. The Buddha said to Subhuti: "What do you think? When the Tathagata was anciently with Dipankara Buddha did he have an attainment in the Dharma?"

"No, World-honoured One, he did not. The Tathagata while with Dipankara Buddha had no attainment whatever in the Dharma."

"Subhuti, what do you think? Does a Bodhisattva set any Buddha-land in array?"

"No, World-honoured One, he does not."

"Why? Because to set a Buddha-land in array is not to set it in array, and therefore it is known as setting it in array. Therefore, Subhuti, all the Bodhisattva-Mahasattvas should thus rouse a pure thought. They should not cherish any thought dwelling on form; they should not cherish any thought dwelling on sound, odour, taste, touch, and quality; they should cherish thoughts dwelling on nothing whatever. Subhuti, it is like unto a human body equal in size to Mount Sumeru; what do you think? Is not this body large?"

Subhuti said: "Very large indeed, World-honoured One. Why? Because the Buddha teaches that that which is no-body is known as a large body."

11. "Subhuti, regarding the sands of the Ganga, suppose there are as many Ganga rivers as those sands, what do you think? Are not the sands of all those Ganga rivers many?"

Subhuti said: "Very many, indeed, World-honoured One."

"Considering such Gangas alone, they must be said to be numberless; how much more the sands of all those Ganga rivers! Subhuti, I will truly ask you now. If there is a good man or a good woman who, filling all the worlds in the three thousand chiliocosms—all the worlds as many as the sands of these Ganga rivers—with the seven precious treasures, uses them all for charity, would not this merit be very large?"

Subhuti said: "Very large indeed, World-honoured One."

Buddha said to Subhuti: "If a good man or a good woman holding even four lines from this sutra preach it to others, this merit is much larger than the preceding one.

12. "Again, Subhuti, wherever this sutra or even four lines of it are preached, this place will be respected by all beings including Devas, Asuras, etc., as if it were the Buddha's own shrine or chaitya; how much more a person who can hold and recite this sutra! Subhuti, you should know that such a person achieves the highest, foremost, and most wonderful deed. Wherever this sutra is kept, the place is to be regarded as if the Buddha or a venerable disciple of his were present."

13. At that time, Subhuti said to the Buddha: "World-honoured One, what will this sutra be called? How should we hold it?"

The Buddha said to Subhuti: "This sutra will be called the *Vajra-prajna-paramita*, and by this title you will hold it. The reason is, Subhuti, that, according to the teaching of the Buddha, Prajnaparamita is not Prajnaparamita and therefore it is called Prajnaparamita. Subhuti, what do you think? Is there anything about which the Tathagata preaches?"

Subhuti said to the Buddha: "World-honoured One, there is nothing about which the Tathagata preaches."

"Subhuti, what do you think? Are there many particles of dust in the three thousand chiliocosms?"

Subhuti said: "Indeed, there are many, World-honoured One."

"Subhuti, the Tathagata teaches that all these many particles of dust are no-particles of dust and therefore that they are called particles of dust; he teaches that the world is no-world and therefore that the world is called the world.

"Subhuti, what do you think? Is the Tathagata to be recognized by the thirty-two marks [of a great man]?"

"No, World-honoured One, he is not."

"The Tathagata is not to be recognized by the thirty-two marks, because what are said to be the thirty-two marks are told by the Tathagata to be no-marks and therefore to be the thirty-two marks. Subhuti, if there be a good man or a good woman who gives away his or her lives as many as the sands of the Ganga, his or her merit thus gained does not exceed that of one who, holding even one gatha of four lines from this sutra, preaches them for others."

14. At that time Subhuti, listening to this sutra, had a deep understanding of its signification, and, filled with tears of gratitude, said this to the Buddha: "Wonderful, indeed, World-honoured One, that the Buddha teaches us this sutra full of deep sense. Such a sutra has never been heard by me even with an eye of wisdom acquired in my past lives. World-honoured One, if there be a man who listening to this sutra acquires a pure believing heart he will then have a true idea of things. This one is to be known as having achieved a most wonderful virtue. World-honoured One, what is known as a true idea is no-idea, and for this reason it is called a true idea.

"World-honoured One, it is not difficult for me to believe, to understand, and to hold this sutra to which I have now listened; but in the ages to come, in the next five hundred years, if there are beings who listening to this sutra are able to believe, to understand, and to hold it, they will indeed be most wonderful beings. Why? Because they will have no idea of an ego, of a person, of a being, or of a soul. For what reason? The idea of an ego is no-idea [of ego], the idea of a person, a being, or a soul is no-idea [of a person, a being, or a soul]. For what reason? They are Buddhas who are free from all kinds of ideas."

The Buddha said to Subhuti, "It is just as you say. If there be a man who, listening to this sutra, is neither frightened nor alarmed nor disturbed, you should know him as a wonderful person. Why? Subhuti, it is taught by the Tathagata that the first Paramita is no-first-Paramita and therefore it is called the first Paramita. Subhuti, the Paramita of humility (patience) is said by the Tathagata to be no-Paramita of humility, and therefore it is the Paramita of humility. Why? Subhuti, anciently, when my body was cut to pieces by the King of Kalinga, I had neither the idea of an ego, nor the idea of a person, nor the idea of a being, nor the idea of a soul. Why? When at that time my body was dismembered, limb after limb, joint after joint, if I had the idea either of an ego, or of a person, or of a being, or a soul, the feeling of anger and ill-will would have been awakened in me. Subhuti, I remember, in my past five hundred births, I was a rishi called Kshanti, and during those times I had neither the idea of an ego, nor that of a person, nor that of a being, nor that of a soul.

"Therefore, Subhuti, you should, detaching yourself from all ideas, rouse the desire for the supreme enlightenment. You should cherish thoughts without dwelling on form, you should cherish thoughts without dwelling on sound, odour, taste, touch, or quality. Whatever thoughts you may have, they are not to dwell on anything. If a thought dwells on anything, this is said to be no-dwelling. Therefore, the Buddha teaches that a Bodhisattva is not to practise charity by dwelling on form. Subhuti, the reason he practises charity is to benefit all beings.

"The Tathagata teaches that all ideas are no-ideas, and again that all beings are no-beings. Subhuti, the Tathagata is the one who speaks what is true, the one who speaks what is real, the one whose words are as they are, the one who does not speak falsehood, the one who does not speak equivocally.

"Subhuti, in the Dharma attained by the Tathagata there is neither truth nor falsehood. Subhuti, if a Bodhisattva should practise charity, cherishing a thought which dwells on the Dharma, he is like unto a person who enters the darkness, he sees nothing. If he should practise charity without cherishing a thought that dwells on the Dharma, he is like unto a person with eyes, he sees all kinds of forms illumined by the sunlight.

"Subhuti, if there are good men and good women in the time to come who hold and recite this sutra, they will be seen and recognized by the Tathagata with his Buddha-knowledge, and they will all mature immeasurable and innumerable merit.

15. "Subhuti, if there is a good man or a good woman who would in the first part of the day sacrifice as many bodies of his or hers as the sands of the Ganga, and again in the middle part of the day sacrifice as many bodies of his or hers as the sands of the Ganga, and again in the latter part of the day sacrifice as many bodies of his or hers as the sands of the Ganga, and keep up these sacrifices through hundred-thousands of myriads of kotis of kalpas; and if there were another who listening to this sutra would accept it with a believing heart, the merit the latter would acquire would far exceed that of the former. How much more the merit of one who would copy, hold, learn, and recite and expound it for others!

"Subhuti, to sum up, there is in this sutra a mass of merit, immeasurable, innumerable, and incomprehensible. The Tathagata has preached this for those who were awakened in the Mahayana (great vehicle), he has preached it for those who were awakened in the Sreshthayana (highest vehicle). If there were beings who would hold and learn and expound it for others, they would all be known to the Tathagata and recognized by him, and acquire merit which is unmeasured, immeasurable, innumerable, and incomprehensible. Such beings are known to be carrying the supreme enlightenment attained by the Tathagata. Why? Subhuti, those who desire inferior doctrines are attached to the idea of an ego, a person, a being, and a soul. They are unable to hear, hold, learn, recite, and for others expound this sutra. Subhuti, wherever this sutra is preserved, there all beings, including Devas and Asuras, will come and worship it. This place will have to be known as a chaitya, the object of worship and obeisance, where the devotees gather around, scatter flowers, and burn incense.

16. "Again, Subhuti, there are some good men and good women who will be despised for their holding and reciting this sutra. This is due to their previous evil karma

for the reason of which they were to fall into the evil paths of existence; but because of their being despised in the present life, whatever evil karma they produced in their previous lives will be thereby destroyed, and they will be able to attain the supreme enlightenment.

"Subhuti, as I remember, in my past lives innumerable asamkhyeya kalpas ago I was with Dipankara Buddha, and at that time I saw Buddhas as many as eighty-four hundred-thousands of myriads of nayutas and made offerings to them and respectfully served them all, and not one of them was passed by me.

"If again in the last [five hundred] years, there have been people who hold and recite and learn this sutra, the merit they thus attain [would be beyond calculation], for when this is compared with the merit I have attained by serving all the Buddhas, the latter will not exceed one hundredth part of the former, no, not one hundred thousand ten millionth part. No, it is indeed beyond calculation, beyond analogy.

"Subhuti, if there have been good men and good women in the last five hundred years who hold, recite, and learn this sutra, the merit they attain thereby I cannot begin to enumerate in detail. If I did, those who listen to it would lose their minds, cherish grave doubts, and not believe at all how beyond comprehension is the significance of this sutra and how also beyond comprehension the rewards are."[1]

18. The Buddha said to Subhuti: "Of all beings in those innumerable lands, the Tathagata knows well all their mental traits. Why? Because the Tathagata teaches that all those mental traits are no-traits and therefore they are

[1] This finishes the first part of the *Diamond Sutra* as it is usually divided here and passes on to the second part. The text goes on in a similar strain through its remaining section. Indeed, there are some scholars who think that the second part is really a repetition of the first, or that they are merely different copies of one and the same original text, and that whatever variations there are in these two copies are the result of the glosses mixed into the text itself. While I cannot wholly subscribe to this view, the fact is that passages containing similar thoughts recur throughout the whole Prajnaparamita literature. In view of this I quote in the following only such ideas as have not fully been expressed in the first part.

known to be mental traits. Subhuti, thoughts[1] of the past are beyond grasp, thoughts of the present are beyond grasp, and thoughts of the future are beyond grasp."

23. "Again, Subhuti, this Dharma is even and has neither elevation nor depression; and it is called supreme enlightenment. Because a man practises everything that is good, without cherishing the thought of an ego, a person, a being, and a soul, he attains the supreme enlightenment. Subhuti, what is called good is no-good, and therefore it is known as good."

26. "Subhuti, what do you think? Can a man see the Tathagata by the thirty-two marks [of a great man]?"

Subhuti said: "So it is, so it is. The Tathagata is seen by his thirty-two marks."

The Buddha said to Subhuti, "If the Tathagata is to be seen by his thirty-two marks, can the Cakravartin be a Tathagata?"

Subhuti said to the Buddha: "World-honoured One, as I understand the teaching of the Buddha, the Tathagata is not to be seen by the thirty-two marks."

Then the World-honoured One uttered this gatha:

"If any one by form sees me,
By voice seeks me,
This one walks the false path,
And cannot see the Tathagata."

29. "Subhuti, if a man should declare that the Tathagata is the one who comes, or goes, or sits, or lies, he does not understand the meaning of my teaching. Why? The Tathagata does not come from anywhere, and does not depart to anywhere; therefore he is called the Tathagata.

[1] *Citta* stands for both mind and thought. The idea expressed here is that there is no particularly determined entity in us which is psychologically designated as mind or thought. The moment we think we have taken hold of a thought, it is no more with us. So with the idea of a soul, or an ego, or a being, or a person, there is no such particular entity objectively to be so distinguished, and which remains as such eternally separated from the subject who so thinks. This ungraspability of a mind or thought, which is tantamount to saying that there is no soul-substance as a solitary unrelated "thing" in the recesses of consciousness, is one of the basic doctrines of Buddhism, Mahayana and Hinayana.

32. "How does a man expound it for others? When one is not attached to form, it is of Suchness remaining unmoved. Why?

"All composite things (*samskrita*)
Are like a dream, a phantasm, a bubble, and a shadow,
Are like a dew-drop and a flash of lightning;
They are thus to be regarded."

IV

The Lankavatara Sutra

This sutra is said to have been given by Bodhidharma to his chief disciple Hui-k'e as containing the essential teaching of Zen. Since then it has been studied chiefly by Zen philosophers. But being full of difficult technical terms in combination with a rugged style of writing, the text has not been so popular for study as other Mahayana sutras, for instance, the *Pundarika*, the *Vimalakirti*, or the *Vajracchedika*.

The chief interlocutor is a Bodhisattva called Mahamati, and varied subjects of philosophical speculation are discussed against a background of deep religious concern. The topic most interesting for the reader of this book is that of *svapratyatmagati*, i.e. self-realization of the highest truth.

Some of the terms may be explained here: "Birth and death" (*samsara* in Sanskrit) always stands contrasted to "Nirvana". Nirvana is the highest truth and the norm of existence while birth and death is a world of particulars governed by karma and causation. As long as we are subject to karma we go from one birth to another, and suffer all the ills necessarily attached to this kind of life, though it is a form of immortality. What Buddhists want is not this.

"Mind only" (*cittamatra*) is an uncouth term. It means absolute mind, to be distinguished from an empirical mind which is the subject of psychological study. When it begins with a capital letter, it is the ultimate reality on which the entire world of individual objects depends for its value. To realize this truth is the aim of the Buddhist life.

By "what is seen of the Mind-only" is meant this visible world including that which is generally known as mind. Our ordinary experience takes this world for something that has its "self-nature", i.e. existing by itself. But a higher intuition tells us that this is not so, that it is an illusion, and that what really exists is Mind, which being absolute knows no second. All that we see and hear and think of as objects of the vijnanas are what rise and disappear in and of the Mind-only.

This absolute Mind is also called in the *Lankavatara* the Dharma of Solitude (*vivikta-dharma*), because it stands by itself. It also signifies the Dharma's being absolutely quiescent.

There is no "discrimination" in this Dharma of Solitude, which means that discrimination belongs to this side of existence where multiplicities obtain and causation rules. Indeed, without this discrimination no world is possible.

Discrimination is born of "habit-energy" or "memory", which lies latently preserved in the "alayavijnana" or all-conserving consciousness. This consciousness alone has no power to act by itself. It is altogether passive, and remains inactive until a particularizing agency touches it. The appearance of this agency is a great mystery which is not to be solved by the intellect; it is something to be accepted simply as such. It is awakened "all of a sudden", according to Asvaghosha.

To understand what this suddenness means is the function of "noble wisdom" (*aryajnana*). But as a matter of experience, the sudden awakening of discrimination has no meaning behind it. The fact is simply that it is awakened, and no more; it is not an expression pointing to something else.

When the Alayavijnana or the all-conserving consciousness is considered a store-house, or better, a creative matrix from which all the Tathagatas issue, it is called "Tathagata-garbha". The Garbha is the womb.

Ordinarily, all our cognitive apparatus is made to

work outwardly in a world of relativity, and for this reason we become deeply involved in it so that we fail to realize the freedom we all intrinsically possess, and as a result we are annoyed on all sides. To turn away from all this, what may psychologically be called a "revulsion" or "revolution" must take place in our inmost consciousness. This is not however a mere empirical psychological fact to be explained in terms of consciousness. It takes place in the deepest recesses of our being. The original Sanskrit is *paravrittasraya*.

The following extracts are from my English translation (1932) of the original Sanskrit text edited by Bunyu Nanjo, 1923.

XVIII

Further, Mahamati, those who, afraid of sufferings arising from the discrimination of birth and death, seek for Nirvana, do not know that birth and death and Nirvana are not to be separated the one from the other; and, seeing that all things subject to discrimination have no reality, imagine that Nirvana consists in the further annihilation of the senses and their fields. They are not aware, Mahamati, of the fact that Nirvana is the Alayavijnana where a revulsion takes place by self-realization. Therefore, Mahamati, those who are stupid talk of the trinity of vehicles and not of the state of Mind-only where there are no shadows. Therefore, Mahamati, those who do not understand the teachings of the Tathagatas of the past, present, and future, concerning the external world, which is of Mind itself, cling to the notion that there is a world outside what is seen of the Mind and, Mahamati, go on rolling themselves along the wheel of birth and death.

XIX

Further, Mahamati, according to the teaching of the Tathagatas of the past, present, and future, all things are unborn. Why? Because they have no reality, being manifestations of Mind itself; and, Mahamati, as they are not born of being and non-being, they are unborn. Mahamati, all things are like the horns of the hare, horse, donkey, or camel, but the ignorant and simple-minded, who are given up to their false and erroneous imaginations, discriminate things where they are not; therefore, all things are unborn. That all things are in their self-nature unborn, Mahamati, belongs to the realm of self-realization attained by noble wisdom, and does not belong essentially to the realm of dualistic discrimination cherished by the ignorant and simple-minded.

The self-nature and the characteristic marks of body, property, and abode evolve when the Alayavijnana is conceived of by the ignorant as grasping and grasped; and then they fall into a dualistic view of existence where they recognize its rise, abiding, and disappearance, cherishing the idea that all things are born and subject to discrimination as to being and non-being. Therefore, Mahamati, you should discipline yourself therein [i.e. in self-realization].

XXIV

Further again, Mahamati, let the Bodhisattva-Mahasattva have a thorough understanding as to the nature of the twofold egolessness. Mahamati, what is this twofold egolessness? [It is the egolessness of persons and the egolessness of things. What is meant by egolessness of persons? It means that] in the collection of the Skandhas, Dhatus, and Ayatanas there is no ego-substance, nor anything belonging to it; the Vijnana is originated by ignorance, deed, and desire, and keeps up its function by grasping objects by means of the sense-organs, such as the eye, etc., and by clinging to them as real; while a world of objects and bodies is manifested owing to the discrimination that takes place in the world which is of Mind itself, that is, in the Alaya-vijnana.

By reason of the habit-energy stored up by false imagination since beginningless time, this world (*vishaya*) is subject to change and destruction from moment to moment; it is like a river, a seed, a lamp, wind, a cloud; [while the Vijnana itself is] like a monkey who is always restless, like a fly who is ever in search of unclean things and defiled places, like a fire which is never satisfied. Again, it is like a water-drawing wheel or a machine, it [i.e. the Vijnana] goes on rolling the wheel of transmigration, carrying varieties of bodies and forms, resuscitating the dead like the demon Vetala, causing the wooden figures to move about as a magician moves them. Mahamati, a thorough understanding concerning these phenomena is called comprehending the egolessness of persons.

Now, Mahamati, what is meant by the egolessness of things? It is to realize that the Skandhas, Dhatus, and Ayatanas are characterized with the nature of false discrimination. Mahamati, since the Skandhas, Dhatus, and Ayatanas are destitute of an ego-substance, being no more than an aggregation of the Skandhas, and subject to the conditions of mutual origination which are causally bound up with the string of desire and deed; and since thus there is no creating agent in them, Mahamati, the Skandhas are even destitute of the marks of individuality and generality; and the ignorant, owing to their erroneous discrimination, imagine here the multiplicity of phenomena; the wise, however, do not. Recognizing, Mahamati, that all things are devoid of the Citta, Manas, Manovijnana, the five Dharmas, and the [three] Svabhavas, the Bodhisattva-Mahasattva will well understand what is meant by the egolessness of things.

Again, Mahamati, when the Bodhisattva-Mahasattva has a good understanding as regards the egolessness of things, before long he will attain the first stage [of the Bodhisattvahood], when he gets a definite cognition of the imageless. When a definite acquisition is obtained regarding the aspect of the stages [of Bodhisattvahood], the Bodhisattva will experience joy, and, gradually and successively going up the scale, will reach the ninth stage where his insight is perfected, and [finally the tenth stage known as] Great Dharma-megha.

Establishing himself here, he will be seated in the great jewel palace known as "Great Lotus Throne" which is in the shape of a lotus and is adorned with various sorts of jewels and pearls; he will then acquire and complete a world of Maya-nature; surrounded by Bodhisattvas of the same character and anointed like the son of the Cakravarti by the hands of the Buddhas coming from all the Buddha-lands, he will go beyond the last stage of Bodhisattvahood, attain the noble truth of self-realization, and become a Tathagata endowed with the perfect freedom of the Dharmakaya, because of his insight into the egolessness of things. This, Mahamati, is what is meant by the egolessness of all things, and in this you and other Bodhisattva-Mahasattvas should well exercise yourselves.

XXVIII

At that time, Mahamati the Bodhisattva-Mahasattva said this to the Blessed One: Now the Blessed One makes mention of the Tathagata-garbha in the sutras, and verily it is described by you as by nature bright and pure, as primarily unspotted, endowed with the thirty-two marks of excellence, hidden in the body of every being like a gem of great value, which is enwrapped in a dirty garment, enveloped in the garment of the Skandhas, Dhatus, and Ayatanas, and soiled with the dirt of greed, anger, folly, and false imagination, while it is described by the Blessed One to be eternal, permanent, auspicious, and unchangeable. Is not this Tathagata-garbha taught by the Blessed One the same as the ego-substance taught by the philosophers? The ego as taught in the systems of the philosophers is an eternal creator, unqualified, omnipresent, and imperishable.

The Blessed One replied: No, Mahamati, my Tathagata-garbha is not the same as the ego taught by the philosophers; for what the Tathagatas teach is the Tathagata-garbha in the sense, Mahamati, that it is emptiness, reality-limit, Nirvana, being unborn, unqualified, and devoid of will-effort; the reason why the Tathagatas, who are Arhats and Fully-Enlightened Ones, teach the doctrine pointing to the Tathagata-garbha is to make the ignorant cast aside their fear when they listen to the teaching of egolessness and to have them realize the state of non-discrimination and imagelessness.

I also wish, Mahamati, that the Bodhisattva-Mahasattvas of the present and future would not attach themselves to the idea of an ego [imagining it to be a soul]. Mahamati, it is like a potter who manufactures various vessels out of a mass of clay of one sort by his own manual skill and labour combined with a rod, water, and thread, Mahamati, that the Tathagatas preach the egolessness of things which removes all the traces of discrimination by various skilful means issuing from their transcendental wisdom; that is, sometimes by the doctrine of the Tathagata-garbha, sometimes by that of egolessness, and like a potter, by means of various terms, expressions, and synonyms. For this reason, Mahamati, the philosophers' doctrine of an ego-substance is not the same as the teaching of the Tathagata-garbha.

Thus, Mahamati, the doctrine of the Tathagata-garbha is disclosed in order to awaken the philosophers from their clinging to the idea of the ego, so that those minds that have fallen into the views imagining the non-existent ego as real, and also into the notion that the triple emancipation is final, may rapidly be awakened to the state of supreme enlightenment. Accordingly, Mahamati, the Tathagatas who are Arhats and Fully-Enlightened Ones disclose the doctrine of the Tathagata-garbha, which is thus not to be known as identical with the philosopher's notion of an ego-substance.

Therefore, Mahamati, in order to abandon the misconception cherished by the philosophers, you must strive after the teaching of egolessness and the Tathagata-garbha.

XXXV

At that time, Mahamati the Bodhisattva-Mahasattva again said this to the Blessed One:

Pray tell me, Blessed One, about the attainment of self-realization by noble wisdom, which does not belong to the path and the usage of the philosophers;

Which is devoid of [all such predicates as] being and non-being, oneness and otherness, bothness and not-bothness, existence and non-existence, eternity and non-eternity;

Which has nothing to do with the false imagination, nor with individuality and generality; which manifests itself as the truth of highest reality;

Which, going up continuously by degrees the stages of purification, enters upon the stage of Tathagatahood;

Which, because of the original vows unattended by any striving, will perform its works in infinite worlds like a gem reflecting a variety of colours;

And which is manifested [when one perceives how] signs of individuation rise in all things as one realizes the course and realm of what is seen of Mind itself, and thereby I and other Bodhisattva-Mahasattvas are enabled to survey things from the point of view which is not hampered by marks of individuality and generality nor by anything of the false imagination, and may quickly attain supreme enlightenment and enable all beings to achieve the perfection of all their virtues.

Replied the Blessed One: Well done, well done, Mahamati! and again, well done, indeed, Mahamati! Because of your compassion for the world, for the benefit of many people, for the happiness of many people, for the welfare, benefit, happiness of many people, both of celestial beings and humankind, Mahamati, you present yourself before me and make this request. Therefore, Mahamati, listen well and truly, and reflect, for I will tell you.

Assuredly, said Mahamati the Bodhisattva-Mahasattva, and gave ear to the Blessed One.

The Blessed One said this to him: Mahamati, since the ignorant and the simple-minded, not knowing that the world is what is seen of Mind itself, cling to the multitudinousness of external objects, cling to the notions of being and non-being, oneness and otherness, bothness and not-bothness, existence and non-existence, eternity and non-eternity, as having the character of self-substance (*svabhava*), which idea rises from discrimination based on habit-energy, they are addicted to false imaginings.

Mahamati, it is like a mirage in which the springs are seen as if they were real. They are imagined so by the animals who, thirsty from the heat of the season, would run after them. Not knowing that the springs are their own mental illusions, the animals do not realize that there are no such springs. In the same way, Mahamati, the ignorant and simple-minded with their minds impressed by various erroneous speculations and discriminations since beginningless time; with their minds burning with the fire of greed, anger, and folly; delighted in a world of multitudinous forms; with their thoughts saturated with the ideas of birth, destruction, and subsistence; not understanding well what is meant by existent and non-existent, by inner and outer, these ignorant and simple-minded fall into the way of grasping at oneness and otherness, being and non-being [as realities].

Mahamati, it is like the city of the Gandharvas which the unwitted take for a real city, though it is not so in fact. This city appears in essence owing to their attachment to the memory of a city preserved in seed from beginningless time. This city is thus neither existent nor non-existent. In the same way, Mahamati, clinging to the memory (*vasana*) of erroneous speculations and doctrines since beginningless time, they hold fast to ideas such as oneness and otherness, being and non-being, and their thoughts are not at all clear about what is seen of Mind-only.

Mahamati, it is like a man, who, dreaming in his sleep of a country variously filled with women, men, elephants, horses, cars, pedestrians, villages, towns, hamlets, cows, buffalos, mansions, woods, mountains, rivers, and lakes, enters into its inner appartments and is awakened. While awakened thus, he recollects the city and its inner apartments. What do you think, Mahamati? Is this person to be regarded as wise, who is recollecting the various unrealities he has seen in his dream?

Said Mahamati: Indeed, he is not, Blessed One.

The Blessed One continued: In the same way the ignorant and simple-minded who are bitten by erroneous views and inclined towards the philosophers, do not recognize that things seen of the Mind itself are like a dream, and are held fast by the notions of oneness and otherness, of being and non-being.

Mahamati, it is like the painter's canvas on which there is neither depression nor elevation as imagined by the ignorant. In the same way, Mahamati, there may be in the future some people brought up in the habit-energy, mentality, and imagination based on the philosophers' erroneous views; clinging to the ideas of oneness and otherness, or bothness and not-bothness, they may bring themselves and others to ruin; they may declare those people nihilists who hold the doctrine of no-birth apart from the category of being and non-being. They [argue against] cause and effect, they are followers of the wicked views whereby they uproot meritorious causes of unstained purity. They are to be kept away by those whose desires are for things excellent. They are those whose thoughts are entangled in the error of self, other, and both, entangled in the error of imagining being and non-being, assertion and refutation; and hell will be their final resort.

Mahamati, it is like the dim-eyed ones who, seeing a hair-net, would exclaim to one another, saying: "It is wonderful! it is wonderful! Look, O honourable sirs!" And the said hair-net has never been brought into existence. It is in fact neither an entity nor a non-entity, because it is seen and not seen. In the same manner, Mahamati, those whose minds are addicted to discrimination of the erroneous views as cherished by the philosophers, and who are also given up to the realistic ideas of being and non-being, oneness and otherness, bothness and not-bothness, will contradict the good Dharma, ending in the destruction of themselves and others.

Mahamati, it is like a firebrand-wheel which is no real wheel but which is imagined to be of such character by the ignorant, but not by the wise. In the same manner, Mahamati, those whose minds have fallen into the erroneous views of the philosophers will falsely imagine in the rise of all beings [the reality of] oneness and otherness, bothness and not-bothness.

Mahamati, it is like those water-bubbles in a rainfall which have the appearance of crystal gems, and the ignorant taking them for real crystal gems run after them. Mahamati, they are no more than water-bubbles, they are not gems, nor are they not-gems, because of their being so comprehended [by one party] and being not so comprehended [by another]. In the same manner, Mahamati, those whose minds are impressed by the habit-energy of the philosophical views and discriminations will regard things born as non-existent and those destroyed by causation as existent.

XXXVII

Further, Mahamati, there are four kinds of Dhyanas. What are the four? They are: (1) The Dhyana practised by the ignorant, (2) the Dhyana devoted to the examination of meaning, (3) the Dhyana with Suchness for its object, and (4) the Dhyana of the Tathagatas.

What is meant by the Dhyana practised by the ignorant? It is the one resorted to by the Yogins exercising themselves in the discipline of the Sravakas and Pratyekabuddhas, who perceiving that there is no ego-substance, that things are characterized with individuality and generality, that the body is a shadow and a skeleton which is transient, full of suffering, and is impure, persistently cling to these notions which are regarded as just so and not otherwise, and who starting from them successively advance until they reach the cessation where there are no thoughts. This is called the Dhyana practised by the ignorant.

Mahamati, what then is the Dhyana devoted to the examination of meaning? It is the one [practised by those who,] having gone beyond the egolessness of things, individuality and generality, the untenability of such ideas as self, other, and both, which are held by the philosophers, proceed to examine and follow up the meaning of the [various] aspects of the egolessness of things and the stages of Bodhisattvahood. This is the Dhyana devoted to the examination of meaning.

What, Mahamati, is the Dhyana with Tathata for its object? When [the Yogin recognizes that] the discrimination of the two forms of egolessness is mere imagination, and that where he establishes himself in the reality of suchness (*yathabhuta*) there is no rising of discrimination, I call it the Dhyana with Tathata for its object.

What, Mahamati, is the Dhyana of the Tathagata? When [the Yogin], entering upon the stage of Tathagatahood and abiding in the triple bliss which characterizes self-realization attained by noble wisdom, devotes himself for the sake of all beings to the [accomplishment of] incomprehensible works, I call it the Dhyana of the Tathagatas. Therefore, it is said:

There are the Dhyana for the examination of meaning, the Dhyana practised by the ignorant, the Dhyana with Tathata for its object, and the pure Dhyana of the Tathagata.

The Yogin, while in the exercise, sees the form of the sun or the moon, or something looking like a lotus, or the underworld, or various forms like sky, fire, etc.

All these appearances lead him to the way of the philosophers; they throw him down into the state of Sravakahood, into the realm of the Pratyekabuddhas.

When all these are tossed aside and there is a state of imagelessness, then a condition in conformity with Tathata presents itself; and the Buddhas will come together from all their countries and with their shining hands will stroke the head of this benefactor.

LXVIII

At the time, Mahamati the Bodhisattva-Mahasattva asked the Blessed One to explain concerning the deep-seated attachment to the existence of all things and the way of emancipation, saying: Pray tell me, Blessed One, pray tell me Tathagata, Arhat, Fully-Enlightened One, concerning the characteristics of our deep attachment to existence and of our detachment from it.

When I and other Bodhisattva-Mahasattvas understand well the distinction between attachment and detachment, we shall know what is the skilful means concerning them, and shall no more become attached to words according to which we grasp meaning.

When we understand well what is meant by attachment to the existence of all things and the detachment from them we shall destroy our discrimination of words and letters; and, by means of our wisdom (*buddhi*), enter into all the Buddha-lands and assemblies; be well stamped with the stamp of the powers, the self-control, the psychic faculties, and the Dharanis; and, well furnished with the wisdom (*buddhi*) in the ten inexhaustible vows, and shining with varieties of rays pertaining to the Transformation Body, behave ourselves with effortlessness like the moon, the sun, the jewel, and the elements; and hold such views at every stage as are free from all the signs of self-discrimination; and, seeing that all things are like a dream, like Maya, etc., [shall be able to] enter the stage and abode of Buddhahood, and deliver discourses on the Dharma in the world of all beings and in accordance with their needs, and free them from the dualistic notion of being and non-being in the contemplation of all things which are like a dream and Maya, and free them also from the false discrimination of birth and destruction; and, finally, [shall be able to] establish ourselves where there is a revulsion at the deepest recesses [of our consciousness], which is more than words [can express].

Said the Blessed One: Well said, well said, Mahamati! Listen well to me then, Mahamati, and reflect well within yourself; I will tell you.

Mahamati the Bodhisattva-Mahasattva said: Certainly, I will, Blessed One; and gave ear to the Blessed One.

The Blessed One said to him thus: Mahamati, immeasurable is our deep-seated attachment to the existence of all things the significance of which we try to understand with words. For instance, there are the deep-seated attachments to signs of individuality, to causation, to the notion of being and non-being, to the discrimination of birth and no-birth, to the discrimination of cessation and no-cessation, to the discrimination of vehicle and no-vehicle, of Samskrita and Asamskrita, of the characteristics of the stages and no-stages. There is the attachment to discrimination itself, and to that arising from enlightenment the attachment to the discrimination of being and non-being on which the philosophers are so dependent, and the attachment to the triple vehicle and the one vehicle, which they discriminate.

These and others, Mahamati, are the deep-seated attachments to their discriminations cherished by the ignorant and simple-minded. Tenaciously attaching themselves to these, the ignorant and simple-minded go on ever discriminating like the silkworms, which, with their own thread of discrimination and attachment, enwrap not only themselves but others and are charmed with the thread; and thus they are ever tenaciously attached to the notions of existence and non-existence. [But really] Mahamati, there are no signs here of deep-seated attachment or detachment. All things are to be seen as abiding in Solitude where there is no evolving of discrimination. Mahamati, the Bodhisattva-Mahasattva should have his abode where he can see all things from the viewpoint of Solitude.

Further, Mahamati, when the existence and non-existence of the external world are understood to be due to the seeing of the Mind itself in these signs, [the Bodhisattva] can enter upon the state of imagelessness where Mind-only is, and [there] see into the Solitude which underlies the discrimination of all things as being and non-being, and the deep-seated attachments resulting therefrom. This being so, there are in all things no signs of a deep-rooted attachment or of detachment. Here Mahamati, is nobody in bondage, nobody in emancipation, except those who by reason of their perverted wisdom recognize bondage and emancipation. Why? Because in all things neither being nor non-being is to be taken hold of.

Further, Mahamati, there are three attachments deep-seated in the minds of the ignorant and simple-minded. They are greed, anger, and folly; and thus there is desire which is procreative and is accompanied by joy and greed; closely attached to this there takes place a succession of births in the [five] paths. Thus there are the five paths of existence for all beings who are found closely attached [to greed, anger, and folly]. When one is cut off from this attachment, no signs will be seen indicative of attachment or of non-attachment.

V

The Ryogonkyo, or Surangama Sutra[1]

There are in the Chinese Tripitaka two sutras bearing the title, "Surangama", but they are entirely different in contents. The first one was translated into Chinese by

[1] "Sutra of Heroic Deed".

Kumarajiva between 402–412 and consists of two fascicles. The second one in ten fascicles was translated by Paramiti in 705, and this is the one used by the Zen and also by the Shingon. The reason why it is used by the Shingon is because it contains the description of a mandala and a mantram called "Sitatarapatala" (white umbrella), the recitation of which, while practising the Samadhi, is supposed to help the Yogin, as the Buddhas and gods will guard him from the intrusion of the evil spirits. But the general trend of thought as followed in this sutra is Zen rather than Shingon. It was quite natural that all the commentaries of it belong to the Zen school. The terms used here are somewhat unusual—especially those describing the Mind. The sutra is perhaps one of the later Mahayana works developed in India. It treats of highly abstruse subjects. Below is a synopsis of it.

1. The sutra opens with Ananda's adventure with an enchantress called Matanga who, by her magic charm, entices him to her abode. The Buddha, seeing this with his supernatural sight, sends Manjusri to save him and bring him back to the Buddha. Ananda is thoroughly penitent and wishes to be further instructed in the art of controlling the mind. The Buddha tells him that all spiritual discipline must grow out of a sincere heart and that much learning has no practical value in life, especially when one's religious experience is concerned. Ananda had enough learning, but no Samadhi to stand against the influence of a sorceress.

2. The reason why we go through the eternal cycle of birth and death and suffer ills incident to it is our ignorance as to the source of birth and death, that is, because Mind-essence is forgotten in the midst of causal nexus which governs this world of particular objects.

This Mind-essence is variously characterized as something original, mysterious, mysteriously bright, illumining, true, perfect, clear as a jewel, etc. It is not to be confused with our empirical mind, for it is not an object of intellectual discrimination.

Ananda is asked to locate this Mind-essence. But, as his mind moves along the line of our relative experience, he fails to give a satisfactory answer. He pursues objective events which are subject to birth and death; he never reflects within himself to try to find the Mind bright and illumining which makes all his experiences possible.

3. Even the Bodhisattva cannot pick up this mysteriously transparent Essence out of a world of individual things. He cannot demonstrate its reality by means of his discerning intelligence. It is not there. But that the Essence is there is evident from the fact that the eye sees, the ear hears, and the mind thinks. Only it is not discoverable as an individual object or idea, objective or subjective; for it has no existence in the way we talk of a tree or a sun, of a virtue or a thought. On the other hand, all these objects and thoughts are in the Mind-essence, true and original and mysteriously bright. Our body and mind is possible only when thought of in connection with it.

4. Because since the beginningless past we are running after objects, not knowing where our Self is, we lose track of the Original Mind and are tormented all the time by the threatening objective world, regarding it as good or bad, true or false, agreeable or disagreeable. We are thus slaves of things and circumstances. The Buddha advises that our real position ought to be exactly the other way. Let things follow us and wait our commands. Let the true Self give directions in all our dealings with the world. Then we shall all be Tathagatas. Our body and mind will retain its original virtue bright and shining. While not moving away from this seat of enlightenment, we shall make all the worlds in the ten quarters reveal themselves even at the tip of a hair.

5. Manjusri is Manjusri; he is absolute as he is; he is neither to be asserted nor to be negated. All assertions and negations start from the truth of this absolute identity, and this is no other than the originally illuminating Mind-essence. Based on this Essence, all the conditions that make up this world of the senses are fulfilled: we see, we hear, we feel, we learn, and we think.

6. Causation belongs to a world of opposites. It cannot

be applied to the originally bright and illumining Essence. Nor can one ascribe to it "spontaneous activity", for this also presupposes the existence of an individual concrete substance of which it is an attribute. If the Essence is anything of which we can make any statements either affirmative or negative, it is no more the Essence. It is independent of all forms and ideas, and yet we cannot speak of it as not dependent on them. It is absolute Emptiness, *sunyata*, and for this very reason all things are possible in it.

7. The world including the mind is divisible into five Skandha (aggregates), six Pravesha (entrances), twelve Ayatana (seats), and eighteen Dhatu (kingdoms). They all come into existence when conditions are matured, and disappear when they cease. All these existences and conditions take place illusively in the Tathagata-garbha which is another name for the Mind-essence. It is the latter alone that eternally abides as Suchness bright, illumining, all-pervading, and immovable. In this Essence of eternal truth there is indeed neither going nor coming, neither becoming confused nor being enlightened, neither dying nor being born; it is absolutely unattainable and unexplainable by the intellect, for it lies beyond all the categories of thought.

8. The Tathagata-garbha is in itself thoroughly pure and all-pervading, and in it this formula holds: form is emptiness and emptiness is form. *Rupam sunyata, sunyateva rupam.* This being so, the Essence which is the Tathagata-garbha reveals itself in accordance with thoughts and dispositions of all beings, in response to their infinitely-varied degrees of knowledge, and also to their karma. In spite of its being involved in the evolution of a world of multiplicities, the Essence in itself never loses its original purity, brilliance or emptiness, all of which terms are synonymous.

9. The knowledge of an objective world does not come from objects, nor from the senses; nor is it mere accident; nor is it an illusion. A combination of the several conditions or factors is necessary to produce the knowledge. But mere combination is not enough. This combination must take

place in the originally pure, bright, illuminating Essence, which is the source of knowledge.

When this is realized, all the worlds in the ten quarters including one's own existence are perceived as so many particles of dust, floating, rising, and disappearing like foam, in the vast emptiness of space which the one illuminative Mind-essence eternally pervades.

10. The question: When the Tathagata-garbha is in itself so pure and undefiled, how is it possible that we have this world of mountains, rivers, and all other composite forms which are subject to constant changes and transformations?

This doubt comes from not understanding the absolute nature of the purity of the Essence. For by purity is not meant relative purity, which is only possible by establishing a dualistic conception of reality. The Essence is neither in the world nor of the world, nor is it outside the world. Therefore the question, which is based on a dualistic interpretation of reality, is altogether irrelevant when applied to the nature of the Essence and its relation to the world.

Hence this remarkable statement: The Tathagata-garbha, which is mysteriously bright and illuminating as the Mind-Essence, is neither to be identified nor not to be identified [with the world]; it is at once this and not-this.

11. Yajnadatta, a citizen of Sravasti, one morning looked into the mirror and found there a face with the most charming features. He thought his own head disappeared and thereby went crazy. This story is used to illustrate the stupidity of clinging to relative knowledge which rises from the opposition of subject and object. As we cling to it as having absolute value, a world of topsyturviness comes to extend before us. The original bright and charming face is possessed by every one of us only when we realize the fact by reflecting within ourselves, instead of running after unrealities.

12. Now Ananda wants to know how to get into the palatial mansion, which he is told to be his own. He is not in

possession of the key wherewith he can open the entrance door. The Buddha teaches him in this way. There are two methods to effect the entrance, both of which being complementary must be practised conjointly. The one is Samatha and the other Vipasyana. *Samatha* means "tranquillization" and *vipasyana* "contemplation".

By Samatha the world of forms is shut out of one's consciousness so that an approach is prepared for the realization of the final stage of enlightenment. When one's mind is full of confusion and distraction, it is no fit organ for contemplation. By Vipasyana is meant that the Yogin is first to awaken the desire for enlightenment, to be firmly determined in living the life of Bodhisattvahood, and to have an illuminating idea as regards the source of the evil passions which are always ready to assert themselves in the Tathagata-garbha.

13. When this source is penetrated by means of Prajna, the entrance is effected to the inner sanctuary, where all the six senses are merged in one. Let the Prajna penetration enter through the auditory sense as was the case with Kwannon Bosatsu, and the distinctions of the six senses will thereby be effaced; that is to say, there will then take place an experience called "perfect interfusion". The ear not only hears but sees, smells, and feels. All the barriers between the sensory functions are removed, and there is a perfect interfusion running between them; each Vijnana then functions for the others.

The Buddha tells Rahula to strike the bell and asks the assembly what they hear. They all say that they hear the bell. The bell is struck again, and they again say that there is a sound which they hear; and that when the bell ceases to ring there is no sound. This questioning and answering is repeated for a few times, and finally the Buddha declares that they are all wrong, for they are just pursuing what does not properly belong to them, forgetting altogether their inner Essence which functions through those objective mediums or conditions. The Essence is to be grasped and not the hearing, nor the sound. To take the latter for reality is the result of confused mentality. By the practice of Vipasyana this is to be wiped off so that the Mind-essence is always recognized in all the functions of an empirical mind as well as in all the phenomena of the so-called objective world. By thus taking hold of the Mind-essence, there is a "perfect interfusion" of all the six Vijnanas, which constitutes enlightenment.

14. The root of birth and death is in the six Vijnanas and what makes one come to the realization of perfect interfusion is also in the six Vijnanas. To seek enlightenment or emancipation or Nirvana is not to make it something separate from or independent of those particularizing agents called senses. If it is sought outside them, it nowhere exists, or rather it becomes one of particular objects and ceases to be what in itself it is. This is why the unattainability of Sunyata is so much talked about in all the Mahayana sutras.

In the true Essence there is neither *samskrita* (created) nor *asamskrita* (uncreated); they are like Maya or flowers born of hallucination. When you attempt to manifest what is true by means of what is erroneous, you make both untrue. When you endeavour to explain object by subject and subject by object, you create a world of an endless series of opposites, and nothing real is grasped. To experience perfect interfusion, let all the opposites, or knots as they are called, be dissolved and a release takes place. But when there is anywhere any clinging of any sort, and an ego-mind is asserted, the Essence is no more there, the mysterious Lotus fades.

15. The Buddha then makes some of the principal persons in the assembly relate their experience of perfect interfusion. That of Kwannon among them is regarded as most remarkable. His comes from the auditory sense as his name implies. It leads him up to the enlightened state of consciousness attained by all the Buddhas, and he is now Love incarnate. But at the same time he identifies himself with all beings in the six paths of existence whereby he knows all their inner feelings and aspirations reaching up towards the love of the Buddha. Kwannon is thus able to reveal

himself anywhere his help is needed, or to any being who hears him. The whole content of the Kwannon sutra is here fully confirmed.

16. Learning is not of much avail in the study of Buddhism as is proved by the case of Ananda, who being enticed by the magical charm of a courtesan was about to commit one of the gravest offences. In the practice of Samadhi the control of mind is most needed, which is Sila (moral precept). Sila consists in doing away with the sexual impulse, the impulse to kill living beings, the impulse to take things not belonging to oneself, and the desire to eat meat. When these impulses are kept successfully under restraint, one can really practise meditation from which Prajna grows; and it is Prajna that leads one to the Essence when the perfect interfusion of all the six Vijnanas is experienced.

17. We here come to the esoteric part of the *Surangama Sutra* where the establishment of the mandala is described, together with the mantram. In this mandala the Samadhi is practised for three weeks or for one hundred days, at the end of which those richly endowed may be able to realize Srotapannahood.

18. Next follows the description of more than fifty stages of attainment leading to final enlightenment and Nirvana; then effects of various karma by which beings undergo several forms of torture in hell are explained; then the causes are given by which beings are transformed into varieties of evil spirits and of beast forms. They, however, come back to the human world when all their sins are expiated. There are beings who turn into ascetics or heavenly beings.

19. While disciplining himself in meditation the Yogin is liable to be visited by all kinds of evil beings whereby he is constantly assailed by hallucinations of various natures. These are all due to highly-accentuated nervous derangements, and the Yogin is advised to guard himself against them.

When the Yogin has all these mental disturbances well under control, his mind acquires a state of tranquillity in which his consciousness retains its identity through his waking and sleeping hours. The modern psychologist would say that he is no more troubled with ideas which are buried, deeply repressed, in his unconsciousness; in other words, he has no dreams. His mental life is thoroughly clear and calm like the blue sky where there are no threatening clouds. The world with its expansion of earth, its towering mountains, its surging waves, its meandering rivers, and with its infinitely variegated colours and forms is serenely reflected in the mind-mirror of the Yogin. The mirror accepts them all and yet there are no traces or stains left in it—just one Essence bright and illuminating. The source of birth and death is plainly revealed here. The Yogin knows where he is; he is emancipated.

20. But this is not yet all. The Yogin must be philosophically trained with all his experiences and intuitions to have a clear, logical, penetrating understanding of the Essence. When this is properly directed, he will have no more confused ideas introduced by misguided philosophers. Along with the training in Samatha, the cultivation of Vipasyana is to be greatly encouraged.

IV. FROM THE CHINESE ZEN MASTERS

There is a large mass of literature to be called especially Zen because of its style and terminology. Until the time of Hui-neng (Yeno in Japanese) and his immediate disciples, there was not much, as far as literary expressions were concerned, to distinguish treatises specifically on Zen from the rest of Buddhist literature. But as time went on there grew up what is now known as the *Yu-lu* (*goroku* in Japanese), containing the sayings and sermons, "gatha" poems, and other literary works of a Zen master. Strictly speaking, the Yu-lu or Goroku is not limited to Zen. One of the chief characteristics of the Zen Goroku is the free use of colloquial expressions which are not found in the classical literature of China. As long as Zen appeals to one's direct experience, abstraction is too inane for the mind of a master.

FROM THE CHINESE ZEN MASTERS

I

Bodhidharma on the Twofold Entrance to the Tao[1]

There are many ways to enter the Path, but briefly speaking they are of two sorts only. The one is "Entrance by Reason" and the other "Entrance by Conduct".[2] By "Entrance by Reason" we mean the realization of the spirit of Buddhism by the aid of the scriptural teaching. We then come to have a deep faith in the True Nature which is the same in all sentient beings. The reason why it does not manifest itself is due to the overwrapping of external objects and false thoughts. When a man, abandoning the false and embracing the true, in singleness of thought practises the

[1] From *The Transmission of the Lamp*, XXX.

[2] "Entrance by Reason" may also be rendered "Entrance by Higher Intuition", and "Entrance by Conduct", "Entrance by Practical Living".

Pi-kuan[1] he finds that there is neither self nor other, that the masses and the worthies are of one essence, and he firmly holds on to this belief and never moves away therefrom. He will not then be a slave to words, for he is in silent communion with the Reason itself, free from conceptual discrimination; he is serene and not-acting. This is called "Entrance by Reason".

By "Entrance by Conduct" is meant the four acts in which all other acts are included. What are the four? 1. To know how to requite hatred; 2. To be obedient to karma; 3. Not to crave anything; and 4. To be in accord with the Dharma.

1. What is meant by "How to requite hatred"? He who disciplines himself in the Path should think thus when he has to struggle with adverse conditions: "During the innumerable past ages I have wandered through a multiplicity of existences, all the while giving myself to unimportant details of life at the expense of essentials, and thus creating infinite occasions for hate, ill-will, and wrongdoing. While no violations have been committed in this life, the fruits of evil deeds in the past are to be gathered now. Neither gods nor men can foretell what is coming upon me. I will submit myself willingly and patiently to all the ills that befall me, and I will never bemoan or complain. The Sutra teaches me not to worry over ills that may happen to me. Why? Because when things are surveyed by a higher intelligence, the foundation of causation is reached." When this thought is awakened in a man, he will be in accord with the Reason because he makes the best use of hatred and turns it into the service in his advance towards the Path. This is called the "way to requite hatred".

2. By "being obedient to karma" is meant this: There is no self (*atman*) in whatever beings are produced by the interplay of karmaic conditions; the pleasure and pain I suffer are also the results of my previous action. If I am rewarded with fortune, honour, etc., this is the outcome of my past deeds which by reason of causation affect my present

[1] "Wall-gazing".

life. When the force of karma is exhausted, the result I am enjoying now will disappear; what is then the use of being joyful over it? Gain or loss, let me accept the karma as it brings to me the one or the other; the Mind itself knows neither increase nor decrease. The wind of pleasure [and pain] will not stir me, for I am silently in harmony with the Path. Therefore this is called "being obedient to karma".

3. By "not craving (*ch'iu*) anything" is meant this: Men of the world, in eternal confusion, are attached everywhere to one thing or another, which is called craving. The wise however understand the truth and are not like the ignorant. Their minds abide serenely in the uncreated while the body moves about in accordance with the laws of causation. All things are empty and there is nothing desirable to seek after. Where there is the merit of brightness there surely lurks the demerit of darkness. This triple world where we stay altogether too long is like a house on fire; all that has a body suffers, and nobody really knows what peace is. Because the wise are thoroughly acquainted with this truth, they are never attached to things that change; their thoughts are quieted, they never crave anything. Says the Sutra: "Wherever there is a craving, there is pain; cease from craving and you are blessed." Thus we know that not to crave anything is indeed the way to the Truth. Therefore, it is taught not "to crave anything".

4. By "being in accord with the Dharma" is meant that the Reason which we call the Dharma in its essence is pure, and that this Reason is the principle of emptiness (*sunyata*) in all that is manifested; it is above defilements and attachments, and there is no "self", no "other" in it. Says the Sutra: "In the Dharma there are no sentient beings, because it is free from the stain of being; in the Dharma there is no 'self' because it is free from the stain of selfhood." When the wise understand this truth and believe in it, their lives will be "in accordance with the Dharma".

As there is in the essence of the Dharma no desire to possess, the wise are ever ready to practise charity with their body, life, and property, and they never begrudge, they never know what an ill grace means. As they have a perfect understanding of the threefold nature of emptiness, they are above partiality and attachment. Only because of their will to cleanse all beings of their stains, they come among them as of them, but they are not attached to form. This is the self-benefiting phase of their lives. They, however, know also how to benefit others, and again how to glorify the truth of enlightenment. As with the virtue of charity, so with the other five virtues [of the Prajnaparamita]. The wise practise the six virtues of perfection to get rid of confused thoughts, and yet there is no specific consciousness on their part that they are engaged in any meritorious deeds. This is called "being in accord with the Dharma".[1]

II

On Believing in Mind (Shinjin-no-Mei)[2]

1. The Perfect Way knows no difficulties
Except that it refuses to make preferences;
Only when freed from hate and love,
It reveals itself fully and without disguise;

[1] Since this translation from the *Transmission of the Lamp*, two Tun-huang MSS. containing the text have come to light. The one is in the *Masters and Disciples of the Lanka* (*Leng-chia Shihtzu Chi*), already published, and the other still in MS., which however the present author intends to have reproduced in facsimile before long. They differ in minor points with the translation here given.

[2] By Seng-t'san (Sosan in Japanese). Died 606 C.E. Mind=*hsin*. *Hsin* is one of those Chinese words which defy translation. When the Indian scholars were trying to translate the Buddhist Sanskrit works into Chinese, they discovered that there were five classes of Sanskrit terms which could not be satisfactorily rendered into Chinese. We thus find in the Chinese Tripitaka such words as *prajna*, *bodhi*, *buddha*, *nirvana*, *dhyana*, *bodhisattva*, etc., almost always untranslated; and they now appear in their original Sanskrit form among the technical Buddhist terminology. If we could leave *hsin* with all its nuance of meaning in this translation, it would save us from the many difficulties that face us in its English rendering. For *hsin* means "mind", "heart", "soul", "spirit"—each singly as well as all inclusively. In the present composition by the third patriarch of Zen, it has sometimes an intellectual connotation but at other times it can properly be given as "heart". But as the predominant note of Zen Buddhism is more intellectual than anything else, though not in the sense of being logical or philosophical, I decided here to translate *hsin* by "mind" rather than by "heart", and by this mind I do not mean our psychological mind, but what may be called absolute mind, or Mind.

A tenth of an inch's difference,
And heaven and earth are set apart;
If you wish to see it before your own eyes,
Have no fixed thoughts either for or against it.

2. To set up what you like against what you dislike—
This is the disease of the mind:
When the deep meaning [of the Way] is not understood
Peace of mind is disturbed to no purpose.

3. [The Way is] perfect like unto vast space,
With nothing wanting, nothing superfluous:
It is indeed due to making choice
That its suchness is lost sight of.

4. Pursue not the outer entanglements,
Dwell not in the inner void;
Be serene in the oneness of things,
And [dualism] vanishes by itself.

5. When you strive to gain quiescence by stopping motion,
The quiescence thus gained is ever in motion;
As long as you tarry in the dualism,
How can you realize oneness?

6. And when oneness is not thoroughly understood,
In two ways loss is sustained:
The denying of reality is the asserting of it,
And the asserting of emptiness is the denying of it.[1]

7. Wordiness and intellection—

[1] This means: When the absolute oneness of things is not properly understood, negation as well as affirmation tends to be a one-sided view of reality. When Buddhists deny the reality of an objective world, they do not mean that they believe in the unconditioned emptiness of things; they know that there is something real which cannot be done away with. When they uphold the doctrine of emptiness this does not mean that all is nothing but an empty hollow, which leads to a self-contradiction. The philosophy of Zen avoids the error of one-sidedness involved in realism as well as in nihilism.

The more with them the further astray we go;
Away therefore with wordiness and intellection,
And there is no place where we cannot pass freely.

8. When we return to the root, we gain the meaning;
When we pursue external objects, we lose the reason.
The moment we are enlightened within,
We go beyond the voidness of a world confronting us.

9. Transformations going on in an empty world which confronts us
Appear real all because of Ignorance:
Try not to seek after the true,
Only cease to cherish opinions.

10. Abide not with dualism,
Carefully avoid pursuing it;
As soon as you have right and wrong,
Confusion ensues, and Mind[1] is lost.

11. The two exist because of the One,
But hold not even to this One;
When a mind is not disturbed,
The ten thousand things offer no offence.

12. No offence offered, and no ten thousand things;
No disturbance going, and no mind set up to work:
The subject is quieted when the object ceases,
The object ceases when the subject is quieted.

13. The object is an object for the subject,
The subject is a subject for the object:
Know that the relativity of the two
Rests ultimately on one Emptiness.

14. In one Emptiness the two are not distinguished,
And each contains in itself all the ten thousand things;

[1] The Mind = the Way = the One = Emptiness.

When no discrimination is made between this and that.
How can a one-sided and prejudiced view arise?

15. The Great Way is calm and large-hearted,
For it nothing is easy, nothing is hard;
Small views are irresolute,
The more in haste the tardier they go.

16. Clinging is never kept within bounds,
It is sure to go the wrong way;
Quit it, and things follow their own courses,
While the Essence neither departs nor abides.

17. Obey the nature of things, and you are in concord with the Way,
Calm and easy and free from annoyance;
But when your thoughts are tied, you turn away from the truth,
They grow heavier and duller and are not at all sound.

18. When they are not sound, the spirit is troubled;
What is the use of being partial and one-sided then?
If you want to walk the course of the One Vehicle,
Be not prejudiced against the six sense-objects.

19. When you are not prejudiced against the six sense-objects,
You are then one with the Enlightenment;
The wise are non-active,
While the ignorant bind themselves up;
While in the Dharma itself there is no individuation,
They ignorantly attach themselves to particular objects.
It is their own mind that creates illusions—
Is this not the greatest of all self-contradictions?

20. The ignorant cherish the idea of rest and unrest,
The enlightened have no likes and dislikes:
All forms of dualism

Are contrived by the ignorant themselves.
They are like unto visions and flowers in the air;
Why should we trouble ourselves to take hold of them?
Gain and loss, right and wrong—
Away with them once for all!

21. If an eye never falls asleep,
All dreams will by themselves cease:
If the Mind retains its absoluteness,
The ten thousand things are of one Suchness.[1]

22. When the deep mystery of one Suchness is fathomed,
All of a sudden we forget the external entanglements;
When the ten thousand things are viewed in their oneness,
We return to the origin and remain where we ever have been.

23. Forget the wherefore of things,
And we attain to a state beyond analogy;
Movement stopped and there is no movement,
Rest set in motion and there is no rest;
When dualism does no more obtain,
Oneness itself abides not.

24. The ultimate end of things where they cannot go any further

[1] *The Masters and Disciples of the Lanka* also quotes a poetical composition of So-san on "The Mysterious" in which we find the following echoing the idea given expression here:

"One Reality only—
How deep and far-reaching!
The ten thousand things—
How confusingly multifarious!
The true and the conventional are indeed intermingling,
But essentially of the same substance they are.
The wise and the unenlightened are indeed distinguishable,
But in the Way they are united as one.
Desirest thou to find its limits?
How broadly expanding! It is limitless!
How vaguely it vanishes away! Its ends are never reached!
It originates in beginningless time, it terminates in endless time."

Is not bound by rules and measures:
In the Mind harmonious [with the Way] we have the principle of identity,
In which we find all strivings quieted;
Doubts and irresolutions are completely done away with,
And the right faith is straightened;
There is nothing left behind,
There is nothing retained,
All is void, lucid, and self-illuminating;
There is no exertion, no waste of energy—
This is where thinking never attains,
This is where the imagination fails to measure.

25. In the higher realm of true Suchness
There is neither "self" nor "other":
When direct identification is sought,
We can only say, "Not two".[1]

26. In being "not two" all is the same,
All that is is comprehended in it;
The wise in the ten quarters,
They all enter into this Absolute Reason.

27. This Absolute Reason is beyond quickening [time] and extending [space],
For it one instant is ten thousand years;
Whether we see it or not,
It is manifest everywhere in all the ten quarters.

28. Infinitely small things are as large as large things can be,
For here no external conditions obtain;
Infinitely large things are as small as small things can be,
For objective limits are here of no consideration.

29. What is is the same as what is not,

[1] I.e. Tat tvam asi.

What is not is the same as what is:
Where this state of things fails to obtain,
Indeed, no tarrying there.

30. One in All,
All in One—
If only this is realized,
No more worry about your not being perfect!

31. Where Mind and each believing mind are not divided,
And undivided are each believing mind and Mind,
This is where words fail;
For it is not of the past, present, and future.

III

From Hui-neng's Tan-ching[1]

24. *Mahaprajnaparamita* is a Sanskrit term of the Western country; in T'ang it means "great-wisdom (*chih-hui*), other-shore reached". This Truth (*dharma=fa*) is to be lived, it is not to be [merely] pronounced with the mouth. When it is not lived, it is like a phantom, like an apparition. The Dharmakaya of the Yogin is the same as the Buddha.

What is *maha*? *Maha* means "great". The capacity of Mind is wide and great, it is like emptiness of space. To sit with a mind emptied makes one fall into emptiness of indifference. Space contains the sun, the moon, stars, constellations, great earth, mountains, and rivers. All grasses and plants, good men and bad men, bad things and good things, Heaven and hell they are all in empty space. The emptiness of [Self-] nature as it is in all people is just like this.

25. [Self-] nature contains in it all objects; hence it is great. All objects without exception are of Self-nature. Seeing all human beings and non-human beings as they are,

[1] The Tun-huang copy, edited by D. T. Suzuki, 1934. Hui-neng=Yeno, 637–712.

evil and good, evil things and good things, it abandons them not, nor is it contaminated with them; it is like the emptiness of space. So it is called great, that is, *maha*. The confused pronounce it with their mouths, the wise live it with their minds. Again, there are people confused [in mind]; they conceive this to be great when they have their minds emptied of thoughts—which is not right. The capacity of Mind is great; when there is no life accompanying it it is small. Do not merely pronounce it with the mouth. Those who fail to discipline themselves to live this life, are not my disciples.

26. What is *prajna*? *Prajna* is *chih-hui* (wisdom). When every thought of yours is not benighted at all times, when you always live *chih-hui* (=*prajna*, wisdom), this is called the life of Prajna. When a single thought of yours is benighted, then Prajna ceases to work. When a single thought of yours is of *chih*, i.e. enlightened, then Prajna is born. Being always benighted in their minds, people yet declare themselves to be living Prajna. Prajna has no shape, no form, it is no other than the essence (*hsing*) of *chih-hui* (wisdom).

What is *Paramita*? This is a Sanskrit term of the Western country. In T'ang it means "the other shore reached". When the meaning (*artha* in Sanskrit) is understood, one is detached from birth and death. When the objective world (*visaya*) is clung to, there is the rise of birth and death; it is like the waves rising from the water; this is called "this shore". When you are detached from the objective world, there is no birth and death for you; it is like the water constantly running its course: this is "reaching the other shore". Hence *Paramita.*

The confused pronounce [Prajna] with their mouths; the wise live it in their minds. When it is merely pronounced, there is at that very moment a falsehood; when there is a falsehood, it is not a reality. When Prajna is lived in every thought of yours, this is known as reality. Those who understand this truth, understand the truth of Prajna and practise the life of Prajna. Those who do not practise it are ordinary people. When you practise and live it in one thought of yours, you are equal to the Buddha.

Good friends, the passions are no other than enlightenment (*bodhi*). When your antecedent thought is confused yours is an ordinary mind; as soon as your succeeding thought is enlightened, you are a Buddha.

Good friends, Prajnaparamita is the most honoured, the highest, the foremost; it is nowhere abiding, nowhere departing, nowhere coming; all the Buddhas of the past, present, and future issue out of it. By means of Great Wisdom (*ta-chih-hui=mahaprajna*) that leads to the other shore (*paramita*), the five skandhas, the passions, and the innumerable follies are destroyed. When thus disciplined, one is a Buddha, and the three passions [i.e. greed, anger, and folly] will turn into Morality (*sila*), Meditation (*dhyana*), and Wisdom (*prajna*).

27. Good friends, according to my way of understanding this truth, 84,000 wisdoms (*chih-hui*) are produced from one Prajna. Why? Because there are 84,000 follies. If there were no such innumerable follies, Prajna is eternally abiding, not severed from Self-nature. He who has an insight into this truth is free from thoughts, from recollections, from attachments; in him there is no deceit and falsehood. This is where the essence of Suchness is by itself. When all things are viewed in the light of wisdom (*chih-hui=prajna*), there is neither attachment nor detachment. This is seeing into one's Nature and attaining the truth of Buddhahood.

28. Good friends, if you wish to enter into the deepest realm of Truth (*dharmadhatu*), and attain the Prajnasamadhi, you should at once begin to exercise yourselves in the life of Prajnaparamita; you just devote yourselves to the one volume of the *Vajracchedika-prajnaparamita Sutra*, and you will, seeing into the nature of your being, enter upon the Prajnasamadhi. It should be known that the merit of such a person is immeasurable, as is distinctly praised in the sutras, of which I need not speak in detail.

This Truth of the highest order is taught to people of great intelligence and superior endowments. If people of small intelligence and inferior endowments happen to hear it, no faith would ever be awakened in their minds. Why?

It is like a great dragon pouring rains down in torrents over the Jambudipa: cities, towns, villages are all deluged and carried away in the flood, as if they were grass-leaves. But when the rain, however much, falls on the great ocean, there is in it neither an increase nor a decrease.

When people of the Great Vehicle listen to a discourse on the *Vajracchedika* their minds are opened and there is an intuitive understanding. They know thereby that their own Nature is originally endowed with Prajna-wisdom and that all things are to be viewed in the light of this wisdom (*chih-hui*) of theirs, and they need not depend upon letters. It is like rain-waters not being reserved in the sky; but the water is drawn up by the dragon-king out of the rivers and oceans, whereby all beings and all plants, sentient and non-sentient, universally share the wet. All the waters flowing together once more are poured into the great ocean, and the ocean accepting all the waters fuses them into one single body of water. It is the same with Prajna-wisdom which is the original Nature of all beings.

29. When people of inferior endowments hear this "abrupt" doctrine here discoursed on, they are like those plants naturally growing small on earth, which, being once soaked by a heavy rain, are all unable to raise themselves up and continue their growth. It is the same with people of inferior endowments. They are endowed with Prajna-wisdom as much as people of great intelligence; there is no distinction. Why is it then that they have no insight even when listening to the Truth? It is due to the heaviness of hindrance caused by false views and to the deep-rootedness of the passions. It is like an overcasting cloud screening the sun; unless it blows hard no rays of light are visible.

There is no greatness or smallness in Prajna-wisdom, but since all beings cherish in themselves confused thoughts, they seek the Buddha by means of external exercises, and are unable to see into their Self-nature. That is why they are known to be people of inferior endowments.

Those beings who, listening to the "Abrupt" doctrine, do not take themselves to external exercises, but reflecting within themselves raise this original Nature all the time to the proper viewing [of the Truth], remain [always undefiled by] the passions and the innumerable follies; and at that moment they all have an insight [into the Truth]. It is like the great ocean taking in all the rivers, large and small, and merging them into one body of water—this is seeing into one's own Nature. [He who thus sees into his own Nature] does not abide anywhere inside or outside; he freely comes and departs; he knows how to get rid of attaching thoughts; his passage has no obstructions. When one is able to practise this life, he realizes that there is from the first no difference between [his Self-Nature] and Prajnaparamita.[1]

30. All the sutras and writings, all the letters, the two vehicles Major and Minor, the twelve divisions [of Buddhist literature]—these are all set forth because of the people of the world. Because there is wisdom-nature (*chih-hui-hsing*), therefore there is the establishment of all these works. If there were no people of the world, no multitudinous objects would ever be in existence. Therefore, we know that all objects rise originally because of the people of the world. All the sutras and writings are said to have their existence because of the people of the world.

The distinction of stupidity and intelligence is only possible among the people of the world. Those who are stupid are inferior people and those who are intelligent are superior people. The confused ask the wise, and the wise discourse for them on the Truth in order to make the stupid enlightened and have an intuitive understanding of it. When the confused are enlightened and have their minds opened, they are not to be distinguished from the people of great intelligence.

Therefore, we know that Buddhas when not enlightened are no other than ordinary beings; when there is one thought of enlightenment, ordinary beings at once turn into Buddhas. Therefore, we know that all multitudinous objects are every

[1] The text has "the Prajnaparamita Sutra" here. But I take it to mean Prajna itself instead of the sutra.

one of them in one's own mind.[1] Why not, from within one's own mind, at once reveal the original essence of Suchness? Says the *Bodhisattvasila Sutra*: "My original Self-nature is primarily pure; when my Mind is known and my Nature is seen into I naturally attain the path of Buddhahood." Says the *Vimalakirti Sutra*: "When you have an instant opening of view you return to your original Mind."

48. The Great Master died on the third day of the eighth month of the second year of Hsien-t'ien (713 C.E.). On the eighth day of the seventh month of this year he had a farewell gathering of his followers as he felt that he was to leave them forever in the following month, and told them to have all the doubts they might have about his teaching once for all settled on this occasion. As he found them weeping in tears he said: "You are all weeping, but for whom are you so sorry? If you are sorry for my not knowing where I am departing to, you are mistaken; for I know where I am going. Indeed, if I did not, I would not part with you. The reason why you are in tears is probably that you do not yourselves know whither I am going. If you did, you would not be weeping so. The Essence of the Dharma knows no birth-and-death, no coming-and-going. Sit down, all of you, and let me give you a gatha with the title, "On the Absolute":[2]

> There is nothing true anywhere,
> The true is nowhere to be seen;
> If you say you see the true,
> This seeing is not the true one.[3]

[1] The text has the "body", while the Koshoji edition and the current one have "mind".

[2] The title literally reads: "the true-false moving-quiet". "True" stands against "false" and "moving" against "quiet" and as long as there is an opposition of any kind, no true spiritual insight is possible. And this insight does not grow from a quietistic exercise of meditation.

[3] That is, the Absolute refuses to divide itself into two: that which sees and that which is seen.

Where the true is left to itself,
There is nothing false in it, which is Mind itself.
When Mind in itself is not liberated from the false,
There is nothing true, nowhere is the true to be found.

A conscious being alone understands what is meant by "moving";[1]
To those not endowed with consciousness, the moving is unintelligible;
If you exercise yourself in the practice of keeping your mind unmoved, [i.e. in a quietistic meditation],
The immovable you gain is that of one who has no consciousness.

If you are desirous for the truly immovable,
The immovable is in the moving itself,
And this immovable is the [truly] immovable one;
There is no seed of Buddhahood where there is no consciousness.

Mark well how varied are aspects [of the immovable one],
And know that the first reality is immovable;
Only when this insight is attained,
The true working of Suchness is understood.

I advise you, O students of the Truth,
To exert yourselves in the proper direction;
Do not in the teaching of the Mahayana
Commit the fault of clinging to the relative knowledge[2] of birth and death.

Where there is an all-sided concordance of views

[1] "Moving" means "dividing" or "limiting". When the absolute moves, a dualistic interpretation of it takes place, which is consciousness.

[2] *Chih, jnana* in Sanskrit, is used in contradistinction to *Prajna* which is the highest form of knowledge, directly seeing into the Immovable or the Absolute.

You may talk together regarding the Buddha's teaching;
Where there is really no such concordance,
Keep your hands folded and your joy within yourself.

There is really nothing to argue about in this teaching;
Any arguing is sure to go against the intent of it;
Doctrines given up to confusion and argumentation
Lead by themselves to birth and death.

IV

YOKA DAISHI'S "SONG OF ENLIGHTENMENT"[1]

1. Knowest thou that leisurely philosopher who has gone beyond learning and is not exerting himself in anything?
He neither endeavours to avoid idle thoughts nor seeks after the Truth;
[For he knows that] ignorance in reality is the Buddha-nature,
[And that] this empty visionary body is no less than the Dharma-body.

2. When one knows what the Dharma-body is, there is not an object [to be known as such],
The source of all things, as far as its self-nature goes, is the Buddha in his absolute aspect;
The five aggregates (*skandha*) are like a cloud floating hither and thither with no fixed purpose,
The three poisons (*klesa*) are like foams appearing and disappearing as it so happens to them.

[1] Yoka Daishi (died 713, Yung-chia Ta-shih, in Chinese), otherwise known as Gengaku (Hsuan-chiao), was one of the chief disciples of Hui-neng, the sixth patriarch of Zen Buddhism. Before he was converted to Zen he was a student of the T'ien-tai. His interview with Hui-neng is recorded in the *Tan-ching*. He died in 713 leaving a number of short works on Zen philosophy, and of them the present composition in verse is the most popular one. The original title reads: *Cheng-tao Ke*, "realization-way-song".

3. When Reality is attained, it is seen to be without an ego-substance and devoid of all forms of objectivity,
And thereby all the karma which leads us to the lowest hell is instantly wiped out;
Those, however, who cheat beings with their false knowledge,
Will surely see their tongues pulled out for innumerable ages to come.

4. In one whose mind is at once awakened to [the intent of] the Tathagata-dhyana
The six paramitas and all the other merits are fully matured;
While in a world of dreams the six paths of existence are vividly traced,
But after the awakening there is vast Emptiness only and not even a great chiliocosm exists.

5. Here one sees neither sin nor bliss, neither loss nor gain;
In the midst of the Eternally Serene no idle questionings are invited;
The dust [of ignorance] has been since of old accumulating on the mirror never polished,
Now is the time once for all to see the clearing positively done.

6. Who is said to have no-thought? and who not-born?
If really not-born, there is no no-birth either;
Ask a machine-man and find out if this is not so;
As long as you seek Buddhahood, specifically exercising yourself for it, there is no attainment for you.

7. Let the four elements go off your hold,
And in the midst of the Eternally Serene allow yourself to quaff or to peck, as you like;
Where all things of relativity are transient and ultimately empty,

There is seen the great perfect enlightenment of the Tathagata realized.

8. True monkhood consists in having a firm conviction;
If, however, you fail to have it, ask me according to your ideas, [and you will be enlightened].
To have a direct understanding in regard to the root of all things, this is what the Buddha affirms;
If you go on gathering leaves and branches, there is no help for you.

9. The whereabouts of the precious *mani*-jewel is not known to people generally,
Which lies deeply buried in the recesses of the Tathagata-garbha;
The sixfold function miraculously performed by it is an illusion and yet not an illusion,
The rays of light emanating from one perfect sun belong to the realm of form and yet not to it.

10. The fivefold eye-sight[1] is purified and the fivefold power[2] is gained,
When one has a realization, which is beyond [intellectual] measurement;
There is no difficulty in recognizing images in the mirror,
But who can take hold of the moon reflected in water?

11. [The enlightened one] walks always by himself, goes about always by himself;
Every perfect one saunters along one and the same passage of Nirvana;
His tone is classical, his spirit is transparent, his airs are naturally elevated,

[1] The fivefold eye-sight (*cakshus*): (1) Physical, (2) Heavenly, (3) Prajna-, (4) Dharma-, and (5) Buddha-eye.

[2] The fivefold power (*bala*): (1) Faith, (2) Energy, (3) Memory, (4) Meditation, and (5) Prajna.

His features are rather gaunt, his bones are firm, he pays no attention to others.

12. Sons of the Sakya are known to be poor;
But their poverty is of the body, their spiritual life knows no poverty;
The poverty-stricken body is wrapped in rags,
But their spirit holds within itself a rare invaluable gem.

13. The rare invaluable gem is never impaired however much one uses it,
And beings are thereby benefited ungrudgingly as required by occasions;
The triple body[1] and the fourfold jnana[2] are perfected within it,
The eightfold emancipation[3] and the sixfold miraculous power[4] are impressed on it.

14. The superior one has it settled once for all and for ever,
The middling one learns much and holds much in doubt;
The point is to cast aside your soiled clothes you so dearly keep with you;
What is the use of showing off your work before others?

15. Let others speak ill of me, let others spite me;
Those who try to burn the sky with a torch end in tiring themselves out;
I listen to them and taste [their evil-speaking] as nectar;

[1] (1) The Dharma-body, (2) the Body of Enjoyment, and (3) the Body of Transformation.

[2] (1) Mirror-intuition, (2) intuition of identity, (3) knowledge of doing works, and (4) clear perception of relations.

[3] *The Abhidharmakosa*, VIII, gives an explanation of the eight Vimoksha. See La Vallee Poussin's French translation, Chap. VIII, pp. 203–221.

[4] For the six Riddhi, which are the supernatural products of the meditations, see op. cit., VII, 122 *ff*.

All melts away and I find myself suddenly within the
Unthinkable itself.

16. Seeing others talk ill of me, I acquire the chance of
gaining merit,
For they are really my good friends;
When I cherish, being vituperated, neither enmity nor
favouritism,
There grows within me the power of love and humility
which is born of the Unborn.

17. Let us be thoroughgoing not only in inner experience
but in its interpretation,
And our discipline will be perfect in Dhyana as well
as in Prajna, not one-sidedly abiding in Sunyata
(emptiness);
This is not where we alone have finally come to,
But all the Buddhas, as numerous as the Ganga sands,
are of the same essence.

18. The lion-roaring of the doctrine of fearlessness—
Hearing this, the timid animals' brains are torn in
pieces,
Even the scented elephant runs wild forgetting its
native dignity;
It is the heavenly dragon alone that feels elated with
joy, calmly listening [to the lion-roaring of the
Buddha].

19. I crossed seas and rivers, climbed mountains, and
forded freshets,
In order to interview the masters, to inquire after
Truth, to delve into the secrets of Zen;
And ever since I was enabled to recognize the path of
Sokei,[1]
I know that birth-and-death is not the thing I have
to be concerned with.

[1] T'sao-ch'i is the name of the locality where Hui-neng had his monastery, and means the master himself.

20. For walking is Zen, sitting is Zen,
Whether talking or remaining silent, whether moving or standing quiet, the Essence itself is ever at ease;
Even when greeted with swords and spears it never loses its quiet way,
So with poisonous drugs, they fail to perturb its serenity.

21. Our Master, [Sakyamuni], anciently served Dipankara the Buddha,
And again for many kalpas disciplined himself as an ascetic called Kshanti.
[I have also] gone through many a birth and many a death;
Births and deaths—how endlessly they recur!

22. But ever since my realization of No-birth, which quite abruptly came on me,
Vicissitudes of fate, good and bad, have lost their power over me.
Far away in the mountains I live in an humble hut;
High are the mountains, thick the arboreous shades, and under an old pine-tree
I sit quietly and contentedly in my monkish home;
Perfect tranquillity and rustic simplicity rules here.

23. When you are awakened [to the Dharma], all is understood, no strivings are required;
Things of the *samskrita*[1] are not of this nature;
Charity practised with the idea of form (*rupa*) may result in a heavenly birth,
But it is like shooting an arrow against the sky,
When the force is exhausted the arrow falls on the ground.

[1] According to Buddhist philosophy, existence is divided into two groups, *samskrita* and *asamskrita*. The samskrita applies to anything that does any kind of work in any possible manner, while the asamskrita accomplishes nothing. Of this class are space regarded as a mode of reality, Nirvana, and non-existence owing to lack of necessary conditions.

Similarly, [when the heavenly reward comes to an end], the life that follows is sure to be one of fortune.
Is it not far better then to be with Reality which is *asamskrita* and above all strivings,
And whereby one instantly enters the stage of Tathagatahood?

24. Only let us take hold of the root and not worry about the branches;
It is like a crystal basin reflecting the moon,
And I know now what this *mani*-gem is,
Whereby not only oneself is benefited but others, inexhaustibly;
The moon is serenely reflected on the stream, the breeze passes softly through the pines,
Perfect silence reigning unruffled—what is it for?

25. The morality-jewel inherent in the Buddha-nature stamps itself on the mind-ground [of the enlightened one];
Whose robe is cut out of mists, clouds, and dews,
Whose bowl anciently pacified the fiery dragons, and whose staff once separated the fighting tigers;
Listen now to the golden rings of his staff giving out mellifluous tunes.
These are not, however, mere symbolic expressions, devoid of historical contents;
Wherever the holy staff of Tathagatahood moves, the traces are distinctly marked.

26. He neither seeks the true nor severs himself from the defiled,
He clearly perceives that dualities are empty and have no reality,
That to have no reality means not to be one-sided, neither empty nor not-empty,
For this is the genuine form of Tathagatahood.

27. The Mind like a mirror is brightly illuminating and knows no obstructions,
It penetrates the vast universe to its minutest crevices;
All its contents, multitudinous in form, are reflected in the Mind,
Which, shining like a perfect gem, has no surface, nor the inside.

28. Emptiness negatively defined denies a world of causality,
All is then in utter confusion, with no orderliness in it, which surely invites evils all around;
The same holds true when beings are clung to at the expense of Emptiness,
For it is like throwing oneself into a flame, in order to avoid being drowned in the water.

29. When one attempts to take hold of the true by abandoning the false,
This is discrimination and there are artificialities and falsehoods;
When the Yogin, not understanding [what the Mind is], is given up to mere discipline,
He is apt, indeed, to take an enemy for his own child.

30. That the Dharma-materials are destroyed and merit is lost,
Comes in every case from the relative discriminatory mind;
For this reason Zen teaches to have a thorough insight into the nature of Mind,
When the Yogin abruptly by means of his intuitive power realizes the truth of No-birth.

31. A man of great will carries with him a sword of Prajna,
Whose flaming Vajra-blade cuts all the entanglements of knowledge and ignorance;

KWANNON

By Seisetsu Seki, Abbot of the Tenryuji Monastery, Kyoto

BODHIDHARMA
(Ta-mo, Daruma)

I Searching for the Ox

II Seeing the Traces

III Seeing the Ox

IV Catching the Ox

V Herding the Ox

VI Coming Home on the Ox's Back

VII The Ox Forgotten, Leaving the Man Alone

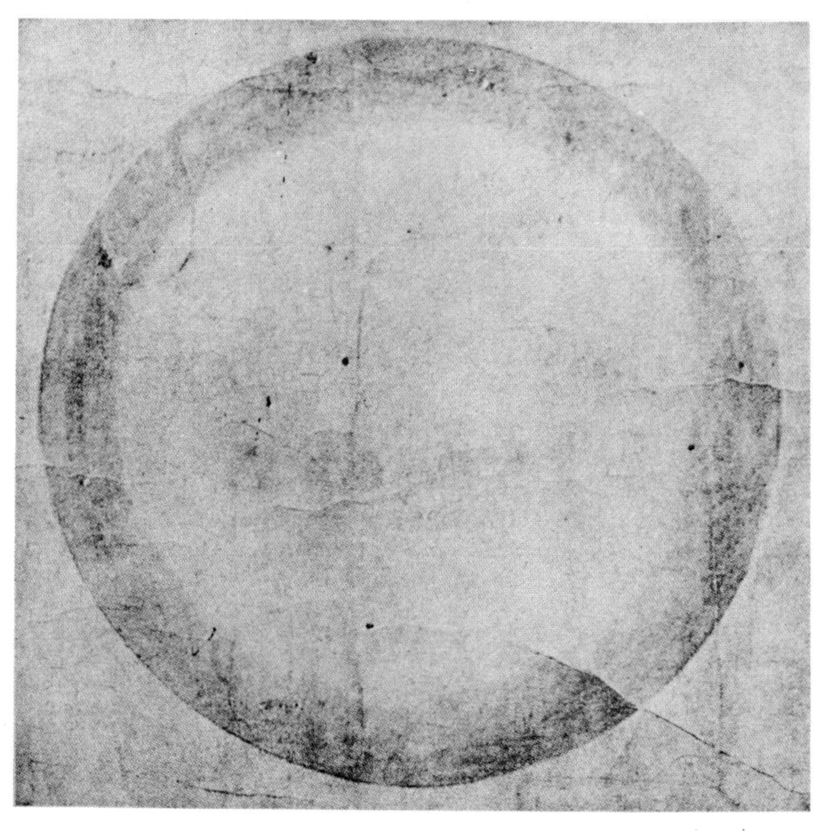

VIII The Ox and the Man Both Gone out of Sight

IX Returning to the Origin, Back to the Source

X Entering the City with Bliss-bestowing Hands

DAITO KOKUSHI
By Hakuin Zenji (See page 145)

HAKUIN ZENJI

Said to have been carved by himself (See page 151)

BHADRAPALA
By Soyen (One of the National Treasures of Engakuji, Kamakura, See page 168)

KANZAN (HAN-SHAN) AND JITTOKU (SHI-TE)
By Kaihoku Yusho
(One of the National Treasures of Myoshinju, Kyoto, See page 182)

It not only smashes in pieces the intellect of the philosophers
But disheartens the spirit of the evil ones.

32. He causes the Dharma-thunder to roar, he beats the Dharma-drum,
He raises mercy-clouds, he pours nectar-showers,
He conducts himself like the lordly elephant or dragon and beings innumerable are thereby blessed,
The three Vehicles and the five Families are all equally brought to enlightenment.

Hini the herb grows on the Himalaya where no other grasses are found,
And the crows feeding on it give the purest of milk, and this I always enjoy.
One Nature, perfect and pervading, circulates in all natures;
One Reality, all comprehensive, contains within itself all realities;
The one moon reflects itself wherever there is a sheet of water,
And all the moons in the waters are embraced within the one moon;
The Dharma-body of all the Buddhas enters into my own being,
And my own being is found in union with theirs.

33. In one stage are stored up all the stages;
[Reality] is neither form, nor mind, nor work;
Even before fingers are snapped, more than eighty thousand holy teachings are fulfilled;
Even in the space of a second the evil karma of three asamkhyeya kalpas is destroyed;
Whatever propositions are made by logic are no [true] propositions,
For they stand in no intrinsic relation to my inner Light.

34. [This inner Light] is beyond both praise and abuse,
Like unto space it knows no boundaries;
Yet it is right here with us ever retaining its serenity and fulness;
It is only when you seek it that you lose it.
You cannot take hold of it, nor can you get rid of it;
While you can do neither, it goes on its own way;
You remain silent and it speaks; you speak and it is silent;
The great gate of charity is wide open with no obstructions whatever before it.

35. Should someone ask me what teaching I understand,
I tell him that mine is the power of Mahaprajna:
Affirm it or negate it as you like—it is beyond your human intelligence;
Walk against it or along with it, and Heaven knows not its whereabouts.

36. I have been disciplined in it for ever so many kalpas of my life;
This is no idle talk of mine, nor am I deceiving you;
I erect the Dharma-banner to maintain this teaching,
Which I have gained at Sokei and which is no other than the one proclaimed by the Buddha.

37. Mahakashyapa was the first, leading the line of transmission;
Twenty-eight Fathers followed him in the West;
The Lamp was then brought over the sea to this country;
And Bodhidharma became the First Father here:
His mantle, as we all know, passed over six Fathers,
And by them many minds came to see the Light.

38. Even the true need not be [specifically] established, as to the false none such have ever been in existence;

When both being and non-being are put aside, even non-emptiness loses its sense;
The twenty forms of Emptiness are not from the first to be adhered to;
The eternal oneness of Tathagatahood remains absolutely the same.

39. The mind functions through the sense-organs, and thereby an objective world is comprehended—
This dualism marks darkly on the mirror;
When the dirt is wiped off, the light shines out;
So when both the mind and the objective world are forgotten, the Essence asserts its truth.

40. Alas! this age of degeneration is full of evils;
Beings are most poorly endowed and difficult to control;
Being further removed from the ancient Sage, they deeply cherish false views;
The Evil One is gathering up his forces while the Dharma is weakened, and hatred is growing rampant;
Even when they learn of the "abrupt" school of the Buddhist teaching,
What a pity that they fail to embrace it and thereby to crush evils like a piece of brick!

41. The mind is the author of all works and the body the sufferer of all ills;
Do not blame others plaintively for what properly belongs to you;
If you desire not to incur upon yourself the karma for a hell,
Cease from blaspheming the Tathagata-wheel of the good Dharma.

42. There are no inferior trees in the grove of sandal-woods,

Among its thickly-growing primeval forest lions alone
find their abode;
Where no disturbances reach, where peace only reigns,
there is the place for lions to roam;
All the other beasts are kept away, and birds do not fly
in the vicinity.

43. It is only their own cubs that follow their steps in the
woods,
When the young ones are only three years old, they
roar.
How can jackals pursue the king of the Dharma?
With all their magical arts the elves gape to no purpose.

44. The perfect "abrupt" teaching has nothing to do with
human imagination:
Where a shadow of doubt is still left, there lies the cause
for argumentation;
My saying this is not the outcome of my egotism,
My only fear is lest your discipline lead you astray
either to nihilism or positivism.

45. "No" is not necessarily "No", nor is "Yes" "Yes";
But when you miss even a tenth of an inch, the difference widens up to one thousand miles;
When it is "Yes", a young Naga girl in an instant
attains Buddhahood,
When it is "No", the most learned Zensho[1] while alive
falls into hell.

46. Since early years I have been eagerly after scholarly
attainment,
I have studied the sutras and sastras and commentaries,
I have been given up to the analysis of names and
forms, and never known what fatigue meant;
But diving into the ocean to count up its sands is surely
an exhausting task and a vain one;

[1] Shang-hsing, lit. "good star", was a great scholar of his age.

The Buddha has never spared such, his scoldings are just to the point,
For what is the use of reckoning the treasures that are not mine?
All my past achievements have been efforts vainly and wrongly applied—I realize it fully now,
I have been a vagrant monk for many years to no end whatever.

47. When the notion of the original family is not properly understood,
You never attain to the understanding of the Buddha's perfect "abrupt" system;
The two Vehicles exert themselves enough, but lack the aspirations [of the Bodhisattva];
The philosophers are intelligent enough but wanting in Prajna;
[As to the rest of us,] they are either ignorant or puerile;
They take an empty fist as containing something real, and the pointing finger for the object pointed;
When the finger is adhered to as the moon itself, all their efforts are lost;
They are indeed idle dreamers lost in a world of senses and objects.

48. The Tathagata is interviewed when one enters upon a realm of no-forms,
Such is to be really called a Kwanjizai (Avalokitesvara):
When this is understood, the karma-hindrances are by nature empty;
When not understood, we all pay for the past debts contracted.

49. A royal table is set before the hungry, but they refuse to eat;
If the sick turn away from a good physician, how are they cured?

Practise Zen while in a world of desires, and the genuine power of intuition is manifested;
When the lotus blooms in the midst of a fire, it is never destroyed.
Yuse (Yung-shih) the Bhikshu[1] was an offender in one of the gravest crimes, but when he had an enlightened insight into No-birth
He instantly attained to Buddhahood and is still living in another world.

50. The doctrine of fearlessness is taught as loudly as a lion roars:
What a pity that confused minds inflexibly hardened like leather
Understand only that grave offences are obstructions to Enlightenment,
And are unable to see into the secrets of the Tathagata's teaching.

51. Anciently, there were two Bhikshus, the one committing murder and the other a carnal offence:
Upali's insight was like that of the glowworm, and ended only in tightening the knots of offence;
But when they were instantly enlightened by the wisdom of Vimalakirti,
Their griefs and doubts melted away like the frost and snow before the blazing sun.

52. The power of incomprehensible emancipation
Works wonders as innumerable as the sands of the Ganga and knows no limits;
[To him] the four kinds of offerings are most willingly made,
By him thousands of pieces of gold are disbursed without involving anybody in debts;
The bones may be crushed to powders, the body cut

[1] The story of this Bhikshu is told in the *Sutra on Cleansing the Karma-hindrances* (*Ching Yeh-chang Ching*).

up to pieces, and yet we cannot repay him enough for what he does for us;
Even a phrase [issuing from him] holds true for hundreds of thousands of kotis of kalpas.

53. He is the Dharma-king deserving the highest respect;
The Tathagatas, as many in number as the Ganga-sands, all testify to the truth of his attainment;
I now understand what this *mani*-jewel is,
And know that all those who accept it in faith are in correspondence [with it].

54. As to seeing it, the seeing is clear enough, but no objects are here to be seen,
Not a person here, nor the Buddha;
Chiliocosms numberless are mere bubbles in the ocean,
All the sages and worthies are flashes of lightning.

55. However rapidly revolves the iron-wheel over my head,
The perfect brightness of Dhyana and Prajna in me is never effaced;
The sun may turn cold and the moon hot;
With all the power of the evil ones the true doctrine remains forever indestructible.
The elephant-carriage steadily climbs up the steepest hill,
Before whose wheels how can the beetle stand?

56. The great elephant does not walk on the hare's lane,
Supreme Enlightenment goes beyond the narrow range of intellection;
Cease from measuring heaven with a tiny piece of reed;
If you have no insight yet, I will have the matter settled for you.

V

Baso (Ma-tsu) and Sekito (Shih-t'ou), Two Great Masters of the T'ang Dynasty

Ma-tsu (Baso) whose posthumous title was the Zen Master of Great Quietude (*ta-chi*) was to be properly called Tao-i (Doichi). His family name was Ma, from the district of Han-chou. His teaching which was originally propagated in the province of Chiang-hsi proved of great influence in the Buddhist world of the time, and he came to be generally known as Ma the Father, that, Ma-tsu.

Historically, Zen Buddhism was introduced to China by an Indian monk called Bodhidharma during the South- and North Dynasties, probably late in the fifth century. But it was not until the time of Hui-neng and Shen-hsiu that Bodhidharma was recognized as the first patriarch of Zen Buddhism in China; for this was the time when Zen to be properly so called came to establish itself as one of the strong Buddhist movements created by Chinese religious genius. The movement firmly took root with Ma-tsu (–788) and Shih-t'ou (700–790). The latter had his monastery in the province of Hu-nan, and thus Hu-nan and Chiang-hsi became the hot-bed of the Zen movement. All the followers of Zen in China as well as in Japan at present trace back their lineage to these two masters of the T'ang.

Shih-t'ou (Sekito) whose family name was Chen came from the district of Tuan-chou. His other name was Hsi-ch'ien. While still young, his religious feeling was strongly stirred against a barbarous custom which was practised among the Liao race. The custom consisted in sacrificing bulls in order to appease the wrath of the evil spirits which were worshipped by the people. Shih-t'ou destroyed many such shrines dedicated to the spirits and saved the victims. He probably acted quite decisively and convincingly so that even the elders of his village failed to prevent him from so rashly working against popular superstitions. He later embraced Buddhism, becoming a disciple of Hui-neng. The latter however died before this young man had been formally ordained as a Buddhist monk. He then went to Hsing-ssu (–740), of Chi-chou and studied Zen Buddhism. Hsing-ssu like Nan-yueh Huai-jang who was the teacher of Ma-tsu, was also a disciple of Hui-neng.

Before quoting Ma-tsu, let me acquaint you with some of Shih-t'ou's questions-and-answers (*mondo*=*wen-to*) as recorded in the *Transmission of the Lamp*.

Hsing-ssu one day asked: "Some say that an intelligence comes from the south of the Ling."

T'ou: "There is no such intelligence from anybody."

Ssu: "If not, whence are all those sutras of the Tripitaka?"

T'ou: "They all come out of here, and there is nothing wanting."

Shih-t'ou, "Stone-head", gains his name because of his having a hut over the flat surface of a rock in his monastery grounds in Heng-chou. He once gave the following sermon: "My teaching which has come down from the ancient Buddhas is not dependent on meditation (*dhyana*) or on diligent application of any kind. When you attain the insight as attained by the Buddha, you realize that Mind is Buddha and Buddha is Mind, that Mind, Buddha, sentient beings, Bodhi (enlightenment), and Klesa (passions) are of one and the same substance while they vary in names. You should know that your own mind-essence is neither subject to annihilation nor eternally subsisting, is neither pure nor defiled, that it remains perfectly undisturbed and self-sufficient and the same with the wise and the ignorant, that it is not limited in its working, and that it is not included in the category of mind (*citta*), consciousness (*manas*), or thought (*vijnana*). The three worlds of desire, form, and no-form, and the six paths of existence are no more than manifestations of your mind itself. They are all like the moon reflected in water or images in the mirror. How can we speak of them as being born or as passing away? When you come to this understanding, you will be furnished with all the things you are in need of."

Tao-wu, one of Shih-t'ou's disciples, then asked: "Who has attained to the understanding of Hui-neng's teaching?"

T'ou: "The one who understands Buddhism."

Wu: "Have you then attained it?"

T'ou: "No, I do not understand Buddhism."

A monk asked: "How does one get emancipated?"

The master said: "Who has ever put you in bondage?"

Monk: "What is the Pure Land?"

Master: "Who has ever defiled you?"

Monk: "What is Nirvana?"

Master: "Who has ever subjected you to birth-and-death?"

Shih-t'ou asked a monk newly arrived: "Where do you come from?"

"From Chiang-hsi."

"Did you see Ma the great teacher?"

"Yes, master."

Shih-t'ou then pointed at a bundle of kindlings and said: "How does Ma the teacher resemble this?"

The monk made no answer. Returning to Ma the teacher, he reported the interview with Shih-t'ou. Ma asked: "Did you notice how large the bundle was?"

"An immensely large one it was."

"You are a very strong man indeed."

"How?" asked the monk.

"Because you have carried that huge bundle from Nan-yueh even up to this monastery. Only a strong man can accomplish such a feat."

A monk asked: "What is the meaning of the First Patriarch's coming from the West?"

Master: "Ask the post over there."

Monk: "I do not understand you."

Master: "I do not either, any more than you."

Ta-tien asked: "According to an ancient sage it is a dualism to take the Tao either as existing or as not-existing. Please tell me how to remove this obstruction."

"Not a thing here, and what do you wish to remove?"

Shih-t'ou turned about and demanded: "Do away with your throat and lips, and let me see what you can say."

Said Ta-tien, "No such things have I."

"If so, you may enter the gate."

Tao-wu asked: "What is the ultimate teaching of Buddhism?"

"You won't understand it until you have it."

"Is there anything over and above it whereby one may have a new turn?"

"Boundlessly expands the sky and nothing obstructs the white clouds from freely flying about."

"What is Zen?" asked a monk.

"Brick and stone."

"What is the Tao?"

"A block of wood."

[1]Someone asked Ma-tsu: "How does a man discipline himself in the Tao?"

The master replied: "In the Tao there is nothing to discipline oneself in. If there is any discipline in it, the completion of such discipline means the destruction of the Tao. One then will be like the Sravaka. But if there is no discipline whatever in the Tao, one remains an ignoramus."

"By what kind of understanding does a man attain the Tao?"

On this, the master gave the following sermon:

"The Tao in its nature is from the first perfect and

[1] The following *mondo* are all taken from a book known as *Sayings of the Ancient Worthies*, fas. I (*Ku tsun-hsiu yu-lu*).

self-sufficient. When a man finds himself unhalting in his management of the affairs of life good or bad, he is known as one who is disciplined in the Tao. To shun evils and to become attached to things good, to meditate on Emptiness and to enter into a state of samadhi—this is doing something. If those who run after an outward object, they are the farthest away [from the Tao].

Only let a man exhaust all his thinking and imagining he can possibly have in the triple world. When even an iota of imagination is left with him, this is his triple world and the source of birth and death in it. When there is not a trace of imagination, he has removed all the source of birth and death, he then holds the unparalleled treasure belonging to the Dharmaraja. All the imagination harboured since the beginningless past by an ignorant being, together with his falsehood, flattery, self-conceit, arrogance, and other evil passions, are united in the body of One Essence, and all melt away.

"It is said in the sutra that many elements combine themselves to make this body of ours, and that the rising of the body merely means the rising together of all these elements and the disappearance of the body means also merely that of the elements. When the latter rise, they do not declare that they are now to rise; when they disappear they do not declare that they are now to disappear.

So with thoughts, one thought follows another without interruption, the preceding one does not wait for the succeeding, each one is self-contained and quiescent. This is called the Sagaramudra-samadhi, "Meditation of the Ocean-stamp", in which are included all things, like the ocean where all the rivers however different in size, etc., empty themselves. In this great ocean of one salt-water, all the waters in it partake of one and the same taste. A man living in it diffuses himself in all the streams pouring into it. A man bathing in the great ocean uses all the waters emptied into it.

"The Sravaka is enlightened and yet going astray; the ordinary man is out of the right path and yet in a way enlightened. The Sravaka fails to perceive that Mind as it is in itself knows no stages, no causation, no imaginations. Disciplining himself in the cause he has attained the result and abides in the Samadhi of Emptiness itself for ever so many kalpas. However enlightened in his way, the Sravaka is not at all on the right track. From the point of view of the Bodhisattva, this is like suffering the torture of hell. The Sravaka has buried himself in emptiness and does not know how to get out of his quiet contemplation, for he has no insight into the Buddha-nature itself.

"If a man is of superior character and intelligence he will, under the instruction of a wise director, at once see into the essence of the thing and understand that this is not a matter of stages and processes. He has an instant insight into his own Original Nature. So we read in the sutra that ordinary beings change in their thoughts but the Sravaka knows no such changes [which means that he never comes out of his meditation of absolute quietude].

" 'Going astray' stands against 'being enlightened'; but when there is primarily no going astray there is no being enlightened either. All beings since the beginningless past have never been outside the Dharma-essence itself; abiding for ever in the midst of the Dharma-essence, they eat, they are clothed, they talk, they respond; all the functioning of the six senses, all their doings are of the Dharma-essence itself. When they fail to understand to go back to the Source they follow names, pursue forms, allow confusing imaginations to rise, and cultivate all kinds of karma. Let them once in one thought return to the Source and their entire being will be of Buddha-mind.

"O monks, let each of you see into his own Mind. Do not memorize what I tell you. However eloquently I may talk about all kinds of things as innumerable as the sands of the Ganges, the Mind shows no increase; even when no talk is possible, the Mind shows no decrease. You may talk ever so much about it, and it is still your own Mind; you may not at all talk about it, and it is just the same your own Mind. You may divide your body into so many forms, and emitting rays of supernatural light perform the eighteen miracles, and yet what you have gained is after all no more than your own dead ashes.

"The dead ashes thoroughly wet have no vitality and are likened to the Sravaka's disciplining himself in the cause in order to attain its result. The dead ashes not yet wet are full of vitality and are likened to the Bodhisattva, whose life in the Tao is pure and not at all dyed in evils. If I begin to talk about the various teachings given out by the Tathagata, there will be no end however long through ages I may go on. They are like an endless series of chains. But once you have an insight into the Buddha-mind, nothing more is left to you to attain.

"I have kept you standing long enough, fare you well!"

P'ang the lay-disciple[1] asked one day when Ma-tsu appeared in the pulpit: "Here is the Original Body altogether unbedimmed! Raise your eyes to it!" Ma-tsu looked straight downward. Said P'ang, "How beautifully the master plays on the first-class stringless lute!" The master looked straight up. P'ang made a bow, and the master returned to his own room. P'ang followed him and said, "A while ago you made a fool of yourself, did you not?"

Someone asked: "What is the Buddha?"

"Mind is the Buddha, and there's no other."

A monk asked: "Without resorting to the four statements and an endless series of negations, can you tell me straightway what is the idea of our Patriarch's coming from the West?"

The master said: "I don't feel like answering it today. You go to the Western Hall and ask Shih-tsang about it."

The monk went to the Western Hall and saw the priest, who pointing at his head with a finger said, "My head aches today and I am unable to explain it to you today. I advise you to go to Brother Hai."

[1] Ho-koji in Japanese. He was one of the greatest disciples of Ma, and for further quotations see my *Essays on Zen*, I, II, and III.

The monk now called on Hai, and Hai said: "As to that I do not understand."

The monk finally returned to the master and told him about his adventure. Said the master: "Tsang's head is black while Hai's is white."

A monk asked: "Why do you teach that Mind is no other than Buddha?"

"In order to make a child stop its crying."

"When the crying is stopped, what would you say?"

"Neither Mind nor Buddha."

"What teaching would you give to him who is not in these two groups?"

"I will say, 'It is not a something.' "

"If you unexpectedly interview a person who is in it what would you do?" finally, asked the monk.

"I will let him realize the great Tao."

The master asked Pai-chang, one of his chief disciples: "How would you teach others?"

Pai-chang raised his *hossu*.

The master remarked, "Is that all? No other way?"

Pai-chang threw the *hossu* down.

A monk asked: "How does a man set himself in harmony with the Tao?"

"I am already out of harmony."

Tan-yuan, one of Ma-tsu's personal disciples, came back from his pilgrimage. When he saw the master, he drew a circle on the floor and after making bows stood on it facing the master. Said Ma-tsu: "So you wish to become a Buddha?"

The monk said: "I do not know the art of putting my own eyes out of focus."

"I am not your equal."

The monk had no answer.

. . . . .

One day in the first month of the fourth year of Chen-yuan (788), while walking in the woods at Shih-men Shan, Ma-tsu noticed a cave with a flat floor. He said to his attendant monk, "My body subject to decomposition will return to earth here in the month to come." On the fourth of the second month, he was indisposed as he predicted, and after a bath he sat cross-legged and passed away.

VI

Huang-po's Sermon, from "Treatise on the Essentials of the Transmission of mind" (Denshin Hoyo)

The master[1] said to Pai-hsiu:

Buddhas and sentient beings[2] both grow out of One Mind, and there is no other reality than this Mind. It has been in existence since the beginningless past; it knows neither birth nor death; it is neither blue nor yellow; it has neither shape nor form; it is beyond the category of being and non-being; it is not to be measured by age, old or new; it is neither long nor short; it is neither large nor small; for it transcends all limits, words, traces, and opposites. It must be taken just as it is in itself; when an attempt is made on our part to grasp it in our thoughts, it eludes. It is like space whose boundaries are altogether beyond measurement; no concepts are applicable here.

[1] Wobaku Ki-un in Japanese, died 850.

[2] One of the first lessons in the understanding of Buddhism is to know what is meant by the Buddha and by sentient beings. This distinction goes on throughout all branches of the Buddhist teaching. The Buddha is an enlightened one who has seen into the reason of existence, while sentient beings are ignorant multitudes confused in mind and full of defilements. The object of Buddhism is to have all sentient beings attain enlightenment like the Buddha. The question is whether they are of the same nature as the latter; for if not they can never be enlightened as he is. The spiritual cleavage between the two being seemingly too wide for passage, it is often doubted whether there is anything in sentient beings that will transform them into Buddhahood. The position of Zen Buddhism is that One Mind pervades all and therefore there is no distinction to be made between the Buddha and sentient beings and that as far as Mind is concerned the two are of one nature. What then is this Mind? Huang-po attempts to solve this question for his disciple Pai-hsiu in these sermons.

This One Mind only is the Buddha, who is not to be segregated from sentient beings. But because we seek it outwardly in a world of form, the more we seek the further it moves away from us. To make Buddha seek after himself, or to make Mind take hold of itself—this is an impossibility to the end of eternity. We do not realize that as soon as our thoughts cease and all attempts at forming ideas are forgotten the Buddha reveals himself before us.

This Mind is no other than the Buddha, and Buddha is no other than sentient being. When Mind assumes the form of a sentient being, it has suffered no decrease; when it becomes a Buddha, it has not added anything to itself. Even when we speak of the six virtues of perfection (*paramitas*) and other ten thousand meritorious deeds equal in number to the sands of the Ganges, they are all in the being of Mind itself; they are not something that can be added to it by means of discipline. When conditions[1] are at work, it is set up; when conditions cease to operate, it remains quiet. Those who have no definite faith in this, that Mind is Buddha and attempt an achievement by means of a discipline attached to form, are giving themselves up to wrong imagination; they deviate from the right path.

This Mind is no other than Buddha; there is no Buddha outside Mind, nor is there any Mind outside Buddha. This Mind is pure and like space has no specific forms [whereby it can be distinguished from other objects]. As soon as you raise a thought and begin to form an idea of it, you ruin the reality itself, because you then attach yourself to form. Since the beginningless past, there is no Buddha who has ever had an attachment to form. If you seek Buddhahood by practising the six virtues of perfection and other ten thousand deeds of merit, this is grading [the attainment of Buddhahood]; but since the beginningless past there is no Buddha whose attainment was so graded. When you get an insight into the One Mind you find there that is no particular reality

[1] *Yuan* in Chinese and *pratyaya* in Sanskrit. One of the most significant technical terms in the philosophy of Buddhism.

[which you can call Mind]. This unattainability is no other than the true Buddha himself.

Buddhas and sentient beings grow out of the One Mind and there are no differences between them. It is like space where there are no complexities, nor is it subject to destruction. It is like the great sun which illumines the four worlds: when it rises, its light pervades all over the world, but space itself gains thereby no illumination. When the sun sets, darkness reigns everywhere, but space itself does not share this darkness. Light and darkness drive each other out and alternately prevail, but space itself is vast emptiness and suffers no vicissitudes.

The same may be said of the Mind that constitutes the essence of Buddha as well as that of sentient being. When you take Buddha for a form of purity, light, and emancipation and sentient beings for a form of defilement, darkness, and transmigration, you will never have the occasion however long [your striving may go on] for attaining enlightenment; for so long as you adhere to this way of understanding, you are attached to form. And in this One Mind there is not a form of particularity to lay your hand on.

That Mind is no other than Buddha is not understood by Buddhists of the present day; and because of their inability of seeing into the Mind as it is, they imagine a mind beside Mind itself and seek Buddha outwardly after a form. This way of disciplining is an error, is not the way of enlightenment.

It is better to make offerings to a spiritual man who is free from mind-attachment[1] than to make offerings to all

[1] *Wu-hsin*, or *mu-shin* in Japanese. The term literally means "no-mind" or "no-thought". It is very difficult to find an English word corresponding to it. "Unconsciousness" approaches it, but the connotation is too psychological. *Mushin* is decidedly an Oriental idea. "To be free from mind-attachment" is somewhat circumlocutionary, but the idea is briefly to denote that state of consciousness in which there is no hankering, conscious or unconscious, after an ego-substance, or a soul-entity, or a mind as forming the structural unit of our mental life. Buddhism considers this hankering the source of all evils moral and intellectual. It is the disturbing agency not only of an individual life but of social life at large. A special article in one of my *Zen Essays* will be devoted to the subject.

the Buddhas in the ten quarters. Why? Because to be free from mind-attachment means to be free from all forms of imagination.

Suchness as it expresses itself inwardly may be likened to wood or rock, it remains there unmoved, unshaken; while outwardly it is like space, nothing is obstructed or checked. Suchness, as it is free both from activity and passivity, knows no orientation, it has no form, there is in it neither gain nor loss. Those who are running [wildly] do not dare enter this path, for they are afraid of falling into an emptiness where there is no foothold to keep them supported. They beat a retreat as they face it. They are as a rule seekers of learning and intellectual understanding. Many are indeed such seekers, like hair, while those who see into the truth are as few as horns.

Manjusri corresponds to *li* (reason or principle) and Samantabhadra to *hsing* (life or action). *Li* is the principle of true emptiness and non-obstruction, *hsing* is a life of detachment from form, and inexhaustible. Avalokitesvara corresponds to perfect love and Sthamaprapta to perfect wisdom. Vimalakirti means "undefiled name"; undefiled is Essence and name is form. Essence and form are not two different things, hence the name Vimala-kirti ("pure-name"). All that is represented by each one of the great Bodhisattvas is present in each of us, for it is the contents of One Mind. All will be well when we are awakened to the truth.

Buddhists of the present day look outward, instead of inwardly into their own minds. They get themselves attached to forms and to the world—which is the violation of the truth.

To the sands of the Ganges the Buddha refers in this way: these sands are trodden and passed over by all the Buddhas, Bodhisattvas, Sakrendra, and other devas, but the sands are not thereby gladdened; they are again trodden by cattle, sheep, insects, and ants, but they are not thereby incensed; they may hide within themselves all kinds of treasures and scented substances, but they are not covetous;

they may be soiled with all kinds of filth and ill-smelling material, but they do not loathe them. A mental attitude of this nature is that of one who has realized the state of *mushin* ("being free from mind-attachment").

When a mind is free from all form, it sees into [the fact] that there is no distinction between Buddhas and sentient beings; when once this state of *mushin* is attained it completes the Buddhist life. If Buddhists are unable to see into the truth of *mushin* without anything mediating, all their discipline of aeons would not enable them to attain enlightenment. They would ever be in bondage with the notion of discipline and merit as cherished by followers of the Triple Vehicle, they would never achieve emancipation.

In the attainment of this state of mind (*mushin*), some are quicker than others. There are some who attain to a state of *mushin* all at once by just listening to a discourse on the Dharma, while there are others who attain to it only after going through all the grades of Bodhisattvaship such as the ten stages of faith, the ten stages of abiding, the ten stages of discipline, and the ten stages of turning-over. More or less time may be required in the attainment of *mushin*, but once attained it puts an end to all discipline, to all realization and yet there is really nothing attained. It is truth and not falsehood. Whether this *mushin* is attained in one thought or attained after going through the ten stages its practical working is the same and there is no question of the one being deeper or shallower than the other. Only the one has passed through long ages of hard discipline.

Committing evils or practising goodness—both are the outcome of attachment to form. When evils are committed on account of attachment to form, one has to suffer transmigration; when goodness is practised on account of attachment to form, one has to go through a life of hardships. It is better therefore to see all at once into the essence of the Dharma as you listen to it discoursed.

By the Dharma is meant Mind, for there is no Dharma apart from Mind. Mind is no other than the Dharma, for there is no Mind apart from the Dharma, This Mind in itself is no-mind (*mushin*), and there is no no-mind either. When no-mind is sought after by a mind, this is making it a particular object of thought. There is only testimony of silence, it goes beyond thinking. Therefore it is said that [the Dharma] cuts off the passage to words and puts an end to all form of mentation.

This Mind is the Source, the Buddha absolutely pure in its nature, and is present in every one of us. All sentient beings however mean and degraded are not in this particular respect different from Buddhas and Bodhisattvas—they are all of one substance. Only because of their imaginations and false discriminations, sentient beings work out their karma and reap its result, while, in their Buddha-essence itself, there is nothing corresponding to it; the Essence is empty and allows everything to pass through, it is quiet and at rest, it is illuminating, it is peaceful and productive of bliss.

When you have within yourself a deep insight into this you immediately realize that all that you need is there in perfection, and in abundance, and nothing is at all wanting in you. You may have most earnestly and diligently disciplined yourself for the past three asamkhyeya kalpas and passed through all the stages of Bodhisattvahood; but when you come to have a realization in one thought, it is no other than this that you are from the first the Buddha himself and no other. The realization has not added anything to you over this truth. When you look back and survey all the disciplinary measures you have gone through, you only find that they have been no more than so many idle doings in a dream. Therefore, it is told by the Tathagata that he had nothing attained when he had enlightenment, and that if he had really something attained, Buddha Dipankara would never have testified to it.

It is told again by the Tathagata that this Dharma is perfectly even and free from irregularities. By Dharma is meant Bodhi. That is, this pure Mind forming the source of all things is perfectly even in all sentient beings, in all the Buddha-lands, and also in all the other worlds together with mountains, oceans, etc., things with form and things without form. They are all even, and there are no marks of distinction between this object and that. This pure Mind, the Source of all things, is always perfect and illuminating and all-pervading. People are ignorant of this and take what they see or hear or think of or know for Mind itself; and their insight is then veiled and unable to penetrate into the substance itself which is clear and illuminating. When you realize *mushin* without anything intervening [that is, intuitively], the substance itself is revealed to you. It is like the sun revealing itself in the sky, its illumination penetrates the ten quarters and there is nothing that will interfere with its passage.

For this reason, when followers of Zen fail to go beyond a world of their senses and thoughts, all their doings and movements are of no significance. But when the senses and thoughts are annihilated, all the passages to the Mind are blocked and no entrance then becomes possible. The original Mind is to be recognized along with the working of the senses and thoughts, only it does not belong to them, nor is it independent of them. Do not build up your views on your senses and thoughts, do not carry on your understanding based on the senses and thoughts; but at the same time do not seek the Mind away from your senses and thoughts, do not grasp the Dharma by rejecting your senses and thoughts. When you are neither attached to nor detached from them, when you are neither abiding with nor clinging to them, then you enjoy your perfect unobstructed freedom, then you have your seat of enlightenment.

When people learn that what is transmitted from one Buddha to another is Mind itself, they imagine that there is a particular object known as a mind which they attempt to grasp or to realize; but this is seeking something outside Mind itself, or creating something which does not exist. In reality, Mind alone is. You cannot pursue it by setting up another mind; however long, through hundreds of thousands of kalpas, you are after it, no time will ever come to you when you can say that you have it. Only when you have an immediate awakening to the state of *mushin* you have your own Mind. It is like the strong man's seeking for his own gem hidden within his forehead: as long as he seeks it outside himself in the ten quarters, he will not come across it; but let the wise once point at it where it lies hidden, and the man instantly perceives his own gem as having been there from the very first.

That followers of Zen fail to recognize the Buddha is due to their not rightly recognizing where their own Mind is. They seek it outwardly, set up all kinds of exercises which they hope to master by degrees, and themselves work out diligently throughout ages. Yet they fail to reach enlightenment. No works compare with an immediate awakening to a state of *mushin* itself.

When you come to a most decided understanding to the effect that all things in their nature are without possessions, without attainments, without dependence, without an abiding place, without mutual conditioning, you will become free from cherishing imagination, which is to realize Bodhi. When Bodhi is realized, your own Mind which is Buddha is realized. All the doings of long ages are then found to have been anything but real disciplining. When the strong man recovered his own gem in his own forehead the recovery had nothing to do with all his efforts wasted in his outside research. So says the Buddha, "I have not had anything attained in my attainment of Enlightenment." Being anxious about our not believing this, he refers to the five eyes[1] and the five statements.[2] But it is truth, not falsehood, for it is the first true statement.

[1] The five eyes are: (1) the physical eye, (2) the heavenly eye, (3) the eye of wisdom, (4) the eye of the Dharma, and (5) the eye of the Buddha.

[2] In the *Diamond Sutra* (*Vajracchedika*), the Buddha makes five statements as regards the truth of his teaching.

VII

Gensha on the Three Invalids[1]

Preliminary Remark

When gates and courts are established, then there are twos, there are threes, there is a realm of multiplicities; when a deep discourse is carried on on the highest subjects of intuition a world of sevens and eights is thoroughly broken through. In whatever ways views and opinions may be presented, they are crushed to pieces so that the barricades even when they are of golden chains are successfully brushed aside. When orders are given from the highest quarters, all traces are wiped off, leaving nothing whereby trailing is made possible. When do we come across such a *koan*? Let one who has an eye on the forehead see to it.[2]

Illustrative Case

Gensha gave the following sermon:

"It is asserted by all the worthy masters of the present time that they are working for the benefit of all beings. [—Each keeps a shop according to his means.—Some are rich and others are poor.]

"This being the case, what will you do if there suddenly appear before you three kinds of invalids? [—By beating up the weeds, we mean to frighten snakes out.—As for me, it makes my eyes open wide and my mouth close.—We all have to beat a retreat even for three thousand *li*.]

"Those who are blind fail to see you even when you

[1] Hsuan-sha, 835-908. The following is a literal translation of Case LXXXVIII of the *Pi-yen Chi*, which is one of the most important and at the same time the most popular of Zen texts. The words in brackets in the "Illustrative Case" and in Seccho's verse are those of Yengo. As to the nature and composition of the *Pi-yen Chi*, see my *Zen Essays*, Series II, p. 237 et seq.

[2] The Remark purposes to make the reader abandon his usual relative point of view so that he can reach the absolute ground of all things.

hold up a mallet or a *hossu*. [—Blind to the very core.—This is no other than 'benefiting all beings'.—Not necessarily failing to see.]

"Those who are deaf fail to hear you even when you talk volubly enough. [—Deaf to the very core!—This is no other than 'benefiting all beings'.—Not necessarily altogether deaf.—That something is still unheard.]

"Those who are dumb fail to speak out, whatever understanding they may have inwardly. [—Dumb to the very core!—This is no other than 'benefiting all beings'.—Not necessarily altogether dumb.—That something is still left untold of.]

"What treatment are you going to accord to such people? If you do not know how to go on with them, Buddhism must be said to be lacking in miraculous works." [—Quite true, this world—I am ready to give myself up with my hands folded.—"Benefiting" already accomplished!—"He then struck."]

A monk asked Ummon (Yun-men) to be enlightened. [—It is also important to go about and inquire.—Hit!]

Said Ummon, "You make bows." [—As the wind blows, the grass bends.—Ch'ua!]

When the monk rose from making bows, [—This monk's staff is broken!]

Ummon poked him with a staff, and the monk drew back. Said Ummon, "You are not blind then?" [—Blind to the very core!—Do not say that this monk has a failing eye-sight.]

Ummon now told him to approach, and the monk approached. [—Washed with a second dipperful of dirty water.—Kwan-non is come! To give a "*Kwatz*!" was better.]

Said Ummon, "You are not deaf then?" [—Deaf to the very core!—Do not say that this monk is deaf in his ears.]

Ummon further continued, "Do you understand?" [—Why does he not feed him with the right forage?—Pity that he then uttered a word at all.]

"No, master, I do not," was the reply. [—A double koan!—What a pity!]

Ummon said, "You are not dumb then?" [—Dumb to the very core!—What eloquence!—Do not say that this monk is dumb.]

The monk now grasped the point. [—Stretching the bow when the burglar is off.—What old bowl is he after?]

Commentary Notes

Gensha gives this sermon from his standpoint where he is now able to sit, after years of his study of Zen, in absolute nakedness with no trumpery trimmings about him, altogether shorn of imaginations and free from conceptualism. In those days there were many Zen monasteries each of which rivalled the others. Gensha used to give this sermon to his monks:

"It is asserted by all the worthy masters of the present time that they are working for the benefit of all beings. This being the case, what will you do if three kinds of invalids suddenly appear before you here? Those who are blind fail to see you even when you hold up a mallet or a *hossu.* Those who are deaf fail to hear you even when you may talk volubly enough. Those who are dumb fail to speak out whatever understanding they may have inwardly. What treatment are you going to accord to such people? If you do not know how to go on with them, Buddhism must be said to be lacking in miraculous works."

If people understand him here as merely making reference to the blind, to the deaf, to the dumb, they are vainly groping in the dark. Therefore, it is said that you are not to search for the meaning in the words which kill; you are requested to enter directly into the spirit itself of Gensha, when you will grasp the meaning.

As Gensha ordinarily tested his monks with this statement, a monk who was staying for some time with him one day accosted him when he came up to the Dharma-hall, and asked: "Will you allow me to present my way of reasoning about your sermon on the three invalids?" Gensha said, "Yes, you may go on." Whereupon the monk remarked,

"Fare thee well, O master!" and left the room. Gensha said, "Not that, not that." We can see that this monk has fully grasped Gensha.

Later on, Hogen (Fa-yen, died 958) made this statement: "When I listened to Master Jizo (Ti-tsang) making reference to this monk's remark, I was enabled to understand Gensha's sermon on the three invalids."

I ask you now. "[Here is a puzzle for you, O monks!] If that monk did not understand Gensha, how was it that Hogen made this statement of his? If that monk understood Gensha, why did the latter declare, 'Not that, not that'?"

One day Jizo said to Gensha, "I am told that you have given a sermon on the three invalids, is that so?" Gensha answered, "Yes." Jizo then said, "I have my eyes, ears, nose, and tongue; what treatment would you give me?" Gensha was quite satisfied with this request on the part of Jizo.

When Gensha is understood, you will realize that his spirit is not to be sought in words. You will also see that those who understand make themselves naturally distinguishable from the rest.

Later when a monk came to Ummon (Yun-men, died 949) and asked him about Gensha's sermon, Ummon was ready to demonstrate it in the following way, for he thoroughly understood Gensha. Said Ummon to the monk, "You make bows." When the monk rose from making bows, Ummon poked him with a staff, and the monk drew back. Said Ummon, "You are not blind then?" Ummon now told him to approach, and the monk approached. Said Ummon, "You are not deaf then?" Finally, he said, "Do you understand?" "No, master," being the reply, Ummon remarked, "You are not dumb then?" This made the monk grasp the point.

If this monk of Ummon's had any sort of understanding about Gensha, he would have kicked up the master's chair when he was told to make bows, and no more fussing would have been necessary. In the meantime let me ask you whether Ummon and Gensha both understood the problem in the same way, or not. I tell you that their understanding is directed to one point. That the ancient masters come out among us and make all kinds of contrivance is because they wish to see somebody bite their hook and be caught up. They thus make bitter remarks in order to have us see into the great event of this life.

My own master Goso (Wu-tsu, died 1104) had this to say: "Here is one who can talk well but has no understanding; here is another who understands but is unable to talk about it. When these two present themselves before you, how will you distinguish the one from the other? If you cannot make this discrimination, you cannot expect to free people from their bondage and attachment. But when you can, I will see to it that, as soon as you enter my gate, I put on a pair of sandals and run through the inside of your body several times even before you realize. In case, however, you fail to have an insight in this matter, what is the use of hunting around for an old bowl? Better be gone!"

Do you wish to know what is the ultimate meaning of these complications in regard to the blind, deaf, and dumb? Let us see what Seccho says about it.

Seccho's Remarks in Verse

Blind, deaf, dumb! [—Even before any word is uttered. —The three sense-organs are perfectly sound.—Already finished is one paragraph!]
Infinitely beyond the reach of imaginative contrivances! [—Where do you wish to hunt for it?—Is there anything here which permits your calculations?—What relationship have they after all?]
Above the heavens and below the heavens! [—Perfectly free is the working of Truth.—Thou hast said!]
How ludicrous! How disheartening! [—What is it that is so ludicrous, so disheartening?—Partly bright and partly dark.]
Li-lou does not know how to discriminate the right colour. [—Blind fellow!—A good craftsman leaves no trace.—Blind to the very core!]

How can Shih-k'uang recognize the mysterious tune? [—Deaf in his ears!—There is no way to appreciate the greatest merit.—Deaf to the very core!]

What life can compare with this?—Sitting alone quietly by the window, [—This is the way to go on.—Do not try to get your livelihood in a cave of ghosts.—Break up all at once this cask of coal tar!]

I observe the leaves fall and the flowers bloom as the seasons come and go. [—What season do you think it is now?—Do not regard this as doing-nothingness.—Today, morning is followed by evening; tomorrow, morning is followed by evening.]

Seccho now remarked: "Do you understand, or not?" [—"Repeated in the gatha."]

An iron bar without a hole! [—Coming up with your own confession!—Too bad that he was released too easily,—"Then he struck."]

Yengo's Comment on Seccho

"Blind, deaf, dumb!
Infinitely beyond the reach of imaginative contrivances!"

In this, Seccho has swept everything away for you—what you see together with what you do not see, what you hear together with what you do not hear, and what you talk about together with what you cannot talk about. All these are completely brushed off, and you attain the life of the blind, deaf, and dumb. Here all your imaginations, contrivances, and calculations are once for all put an end to, they are no more made use of, this is where lies the highest point of Zen, this is where we have true blindness, true deafness, and true dumbness, each in its artless and effectless aspect.

"Above the heavens and below the heavens!
How ludicrous! how disheartening!"

Here Seccho lifts up with one hand and with the other puts down. Tell me what he finds to be ludicrous, what he finds to be disheartening. It is ludicrous that this dumb person is not after all dumb, that this deaf one is not after all deaf; it is disheartening that the one who is not at all blind is blind for all that, and that the one who is not at all deaf is deaf for all that.

> "Li-lou does not know how to discriminate the right colour."

When he is unable to discriminate between blue and yellow, red and white, he is certainly a blind man. He lived in the reign of the Emperor Huang. He is said to have been able to discern the point of a soft hair at a distance of one hundred steps. His eye-sight was extraordinary. When the Emperor Huang had a pleasure-trip to the River Ch'ih, he dropped his precious jewel in the water and made Li fetch it up. But he failed. The Emperor made Ch'ih-kou search for it, but he also failed to locate it. Later Hsiang-wang was ordered to get it, and he got it. Hence:

> "When Hsiang-wang goes down, the precious gem shines most brilliantly;
> But where Li-lou walks about, the waves rise even to the sky."

When we come up to these higher spheres, even the eyes of Li-lou are incapacitated to distinguish which is the right colour.

"How can Shih-kuang recognize the mysterious tune?"

Shih-kuang was son of Ching-kuang of Chin in the province of Chiang in the Chou dynasty. His other name was Tzu-yeh. He could thoroughly distinguish the five sounds and the six notes, he could even hear the ants fight on the other side of a hill. When Chin and Ch'u were at war, Shih-kuang could tell, by merely quietly playing on the strings of his lute, that the engagement would surely be unfavourable for Ch'u. In spite of his extraordinary sensitiveness, Seccho (Hsueh-t'ou) declares that he is unable to recognize the mysterious tune. After all, one who is not at all deaf is really deaf in his ears. The most exquisite note in the higher spheres is indeed beyond the ear of Shih-kuang. Says Seccho: "I am not going to be a Li-lou, nor to be a Shih-kuang, but

> "What life can compare with this?—Sitting alone quietly by the window,
> I observe the leaves fall, the flowers bloom as the seasons come and go."

When one attains this stage of realization, seeing is no-seeing, hearing is no-hearing, preaching is no-preaching. When hungry one eats, when tired one sleeps. Let the leaves fall, let the flowers bloom as they like. When the leaves fall, I know it is the autumn; when the flowers bloom, I know it is the spring. Each season has its own features.

Having swept everything clean before you, Seccho now opens a passageway, saying: "Do you understand, or not?" He has done all he could for you, he is exhausted, only able to turn about and present to you this iron-bar without a hole. It is a most significant expression. Look and see with your own eyes! If you hesitate, you miss the mark for ever.

Yengo (Yuan-wu, the author of this commentary note) now raised his *hossu* and said, "Do you see?" He then struck his chair and said, "Do you hear?" Coming down from the chair, he said, "Was anything talked about?"

VIII

The Ten Oxherding Pictures

Preliminary

The author of these "Ten Oxherding Pictures" is said to be a Zen master of the Sung Dynasty known as Kaku-an Shi-en (Kuo-an Shih-yuan) belonging to the Rinzai school. He is also the author of the poems and introductory words attached to the pictures. He was not however the first who attempted to illustrate by means of pictures stages of Zen discipline, for in his general preface to the pictures he refers to another Zen master called Seikyo (Ching-chu), probably a contemporary of his, who made use of the ox to explain his Zen teaching. But in Seikyo's case the gradual development of the Zen life was indicated by a progressive whitening of the animal, ending in the disappearance of the whole being. There were in this only five pictures, instead of ten as by Kaku-an. Kaku-an thought this was somewhat misleading because of an empty circle being made the goal of Zen discipline. Some might take mere emptiness as all important and final. Hence his improvement resulting in the "Ten Oxherding Pictures" as we have them now.

According to a commentator of Kaku-an's Pictures, there is another series of the Oxherding Pictures by a Zen master called Jitoku Ki (Tzu-te Hui), who apparently knew of the existence of the Five Pictures by Seikyo, for Jitoku's are six in number. The last one, No. 6, goes beyond the stage of absolute emptiness where Seikyo's end: the poem reads:

"Even beyond the ultimate limits there extends a passageway,
Whereby he comes back among the six realms of existence;
Every worldly affair is a Buddhist work,
And wherever he goes he finds his home air;
Like a gem he stands out even in the mud,
Like pure gold he shines even in the furnace;
Along the endless road [of birth and death] he walks sufficient unto himself,
In whatever associations he is found he moves leisurely unattached."

Jitoku's ox grows whiter as Seikyo's, and in this particular respect both differ from Kaku-an's conception. In the latter there is no whitening process. In Japan Kaku-an's Ten Pictures gained a wide circulation, and at present all the oxherding books reproduce them. The earliest one belongs I think to the fifteenth century. In China however a different edition seems to have been in vogue, one belonging to the

Seikyo and Jitoku series of pictures. The author is not known. The edition containing the preface by Chu-hung, 1585, has ten pictures, each of which is preceded by Pu-ming's poem. As to who this Pu-ming was, Chu-hung himself professes ignorance. In these pictures the ox's colouring changes together with the oxherd's management of him. The quaint original Chinese prints are reproduced below, and also Pu-ming's verses translated into English.

Thus as far as I can identify there are four varieties of the Oxherding Pictures: (1) by Kaku-an, (2) by Seikyo, (3) by Jitoku, and (4) by an unknown author.

Kaku-an's "Pictures" here reproduced are by Shubun, a Zen priest of the fifteenth century. The original pictures are preserved at Shokokuji, Kyoto. He was one of the greatest painters in black and white in the Ashikaga period.

The Ten Oxherding Pictures, I.
by Kaku-an

I

Searching for the Ox. The beast has never gone astray, and what is the use of searching for him? The reason why the oxherd is not on intimate terms with him is because the oxherd himself has violated his own inmost nature. The beast is lost, for the oxherd has himself been led out of the way through his deluding senses. His home is receding farther away from him, and byways and crossways are ever confused. Desire for gain and fear of loss burn like fire; ideas of right and wrong shoot up like a phalanx.

Alone in the wilderness, lost in the jungle, the boy is searching, searching!
The swelling waters, the far-away mountains, and the unending path;
Exhausted and in despair, he knows not where to go,
He only hears the evening cicadas singing in the maple-woods.

II

Seeing the Traces. By the aid of the sutras and by inquiring into the doctrines, he has come to understand something, he has found the traces. He now knows that vessels, however varied, are all of gold, and that the objective world is a reflection of the Self. Yet, he is unable to distinguish what is good from what is not, his mind is still confused as to truth and falsehood. As he has not yet entered the gate, he is provisionally said to have noticed the traces.

By the stream and under the trees, scattered are the traces of the lost;
The sweet-scented grasses are growing thick—did he find the way?
However remote over the hills and far away the beast may wander,
His nose reaches the heavens and none can conceal it.

III

Seeing the Ox. The boy finds the way by the sound he hears; he sees thereby into the origin of things, and all his senses are in harmonious order. In all his activities, it is manifestly present. It is like the salt in water and the glue in colour. [It is there though not distinguishable as an individual entity.] When the eye is properly directed, he will find that it is no other than himself.

On a yonder branch perches a nightingale cheerfully singing;
The sun is warm, and a soothing breeze blows, on the bank the willows are green;
The ox is there all by himself, nowhere is he to hide himself;
The splendid head decorated with stately horns—what painter can reproduce him?

IV

Catching the Ox. Long lost in the wilderness, the boy has at last found the ox and his hands are on him. But, owing to the overwhelming pressure of the outside world, the ox is hard to keep under control. He constantly longs for the old sweet-scented field. The wild nature is still unruly, and altogether refuses to be broken. If the oxherd wishes to see the ox completely in harmony with himself, he has surely to use the whip freely.

With the energy of his whole being, the boy has at last taken hold of the ox:
But how wild his will, how ungovernable his power!
At times he struts up a plateau,
When lo! he is lost again in a misty unpenetrable mountain-pass.

V

Herding the Ox. When a thought moves, another follows, and then another—an endless train of thoughts is thus awakened. Through enlightenment all this turns into truth; but falsehood asserts itself when confusion prevails. Things oppress us not because of an objective world, but because of a self-deceiving mind. Do not let the nose-string loose, hold it tight, and allow no vacillation.

The boy is not to separate himself with his whip and tether,
Lest the animal should wander away into a world of defilements;
When he is properly tended to, he will grow pure and docile;
Without a chain, nothing binding, he will by himself follow the oxherd.

VI

Coming Home on the Ox's Back. The struggle is over; the man is no more concerned with gain and loss. He hums a rustic tune of the woodman, he sings simple songs of the village-boy. Saddling himself on the ox's back, his eyes are fixed on things not of the earth, earthy. Even if he is called, he will not turn his head; however enticed he will no more be kept back.

Riding on the animal, he leisurely wends his way home:
Enveloped in the evening mist, how tunefully the flute vanishes away!
Singing a ditty, beating time, his heart is filled with a joy indescribable!
That he is now one of those who know, need it be told?

VII

The Ox Forgotten, Leaving the Man Alone. The dharmas are one and the ox is symbolic. When you know that what you need is not the snare or set-net but the hare or fish, it is like gold separated from the dross, it is like the moon rising out of the clouds. The one ray of light serene and penetrating shines even before days of creation.

Riding on the animal, he is at last back in his home,
Where lo! the ox is no more; the man alone sits serenely.
Though the red sun is high up in the sky, he is still quietly dreaming,
Under a straw-thatched roof are his whip and rope idly lying.

VIII

The Ox and the Man Both Gone out of Sight.[1] All confusion is set aside, and serenity alone prevails; even the idea of holiness does not obtain. He does not linger about where the Buddha is, and as to where there is no Buddha he speedily passes by. When there exists no form of dualism, even a thousand-eyed one fails to detect a loop-hole. A holiness before which birds offer flowers is but a farce.

All is empty—the whip, the rope, the man, and the ox:
Who can ever survey the vastness of heaven?
Over the furnace burning ablaze, not a flake of snow can fall:
When this state of things obtains, manifest is the spirit of the ancient master.

IX

Returning to the Origin, Back to the Source. From the very beginning, pure and immaculate, the man has never been affected by defilement. He watches the growth of things, while himself abiding in the immovable serenity of non-assertion. He does not identify himself with the maya-like transformations [that are going on about him], nor has he any use of himself [which is artificiality]. The waters are blue, the mountains are green; sitting alone, he observes things undergoing changes.

[1] It will be interesting to note what a mystic philosopher has to say about this: "A man shall become truly poor and as free from his creature will as he was when he was born. And I say to you, by the eternal truth, that as long as ye desire to fulfil the will of God, and have any desire after eternity and God; so long are ye not truly poor. He alone hath true spiritual poverty who wills nothing, knows nothing, desires nothing."—(From Eckhart as quoted by Inge in *Light, Life, and Love.*)

To return to the Origin, to be back at the Source—
already a false step this!
Far better it is to stay at home, blind and deaf, and
without much ado;
Sitting in the hut, he takes no cognisance of things
outside,
Behold the streams flowing—whither nobody knows;
and the flowers vividly red—for whom are they?

X

Entering the City with Bliss-bestowing Hands. His thatched cottage gate is closed, and even the wisest know him not. No glimpses of his inner life are to be caught; for he goes on his own way without following the steps of the ancient sages. Carrying a gourd[1] he goes out into the market, leaning against a staff[2] he comes home. He is found in company with wine-bibbers and butchers, he and they are all converted into Buddhas.

Bare-chested and bare-footed, he comes out into the
market-place;
Daubed with mud and ashes, how broadly he smiles!
There is no need for the miraculous power of the gods,
For he touches, and lo! the dead trees are in full
bloom.

[1] Symbol of emptiness (*sunyata*).

[2] No extra property he has, for he knows that the desire to possess is the curse of human life.

The Ten Oxherding Pictures, II.

1. *Undisciplined*

With his horns fiercely projected in the air the beast snorts,
Madly running over the mountain paths, farther and farther he goes astray!
A dark cloud is spread across the entrance of the valley,
And who knows how much of the fine fresh herb is trampled under his wild hoofs!

2. *Discipline Begun*

I am in possession of a straw rope, and I pass it
through his nose,
For once he makes a frantic attempt to run away, but
he is severely whipped and whipped;
The beast resists the training with all the power there
is in a nature wild and ungoverned,
But the rustic oxherd never relaxes his pulling tether
and ever-ready whip.

3. *In Harness*

Gradually getting into harness the beast is now content to be led by the nose,
Crossing the stream, walking along the mountain path, he follows every step of the leader;
The leader holds the rope tightly in his hand never letting it go,
All day long he is on the alert almost unconscious of what fatigue is.

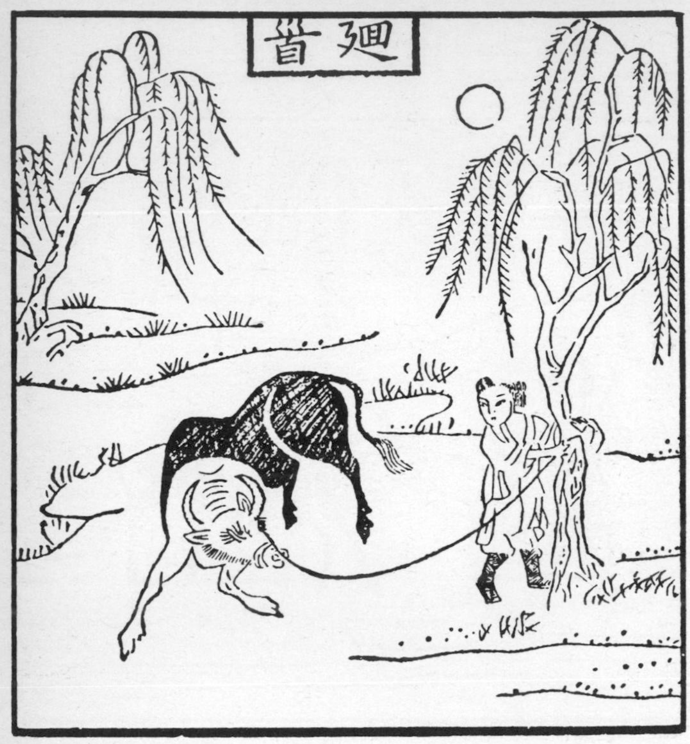

4. *Faced Round*

After long days of training the result begins to tell and the beast is faced round,
A nature so wild and ungoverned is finally broken, he has become gentler;
But the tender has not yet given him his full confidence,
He still keeps his straw rope with which the ox is now tied to a tree.

5. *Tamed*

Under the green willow tree and by the ancient mountain stream,
The ox is set at liberty to pursue his own pleasures;
At the eventide when a grey mist descends on the pasture,
The boy wends his homeward way with the animal quietly following.

6. *Unimpeded*

On the verdant field the beast contentedly lies idling
his time away,
No whip is needed now, nor any kind of restraint;
The boy too sits leisurely under the pine tree,
Playing a tune of peace, overflowing with joy.

7. *Laissez Faire*

The spring stream in the evening sun flows languidly along the willow-lined bank,
In the hazy atmosphere the meadow grass is seen growing thick;
When hungry he grazes, when thirsty he quaffs, as time sweetly slides,
While the boy on the rock dozes for hours not noticing anything that goes on about him.

8. *All Forgotten*

The beast all in white now is surrounded by the white clouds,
The man is perfectly at his ease and care-free, so is his companion;
The white clouds penetrated by the moon-light cast their white shadows below,
The white clouds and the bright moon-light—each following its course of movement.

9. *The Solitary Moon*

Nowhere is the beast, and the oxherd is master of his
 time,
He is a solitary cloud wafting lightly along the
 mountain peaks;
Clapping his hands he sings joyfully in the moon-light,
But remember a last wall is still left barring his
 homeward walk.

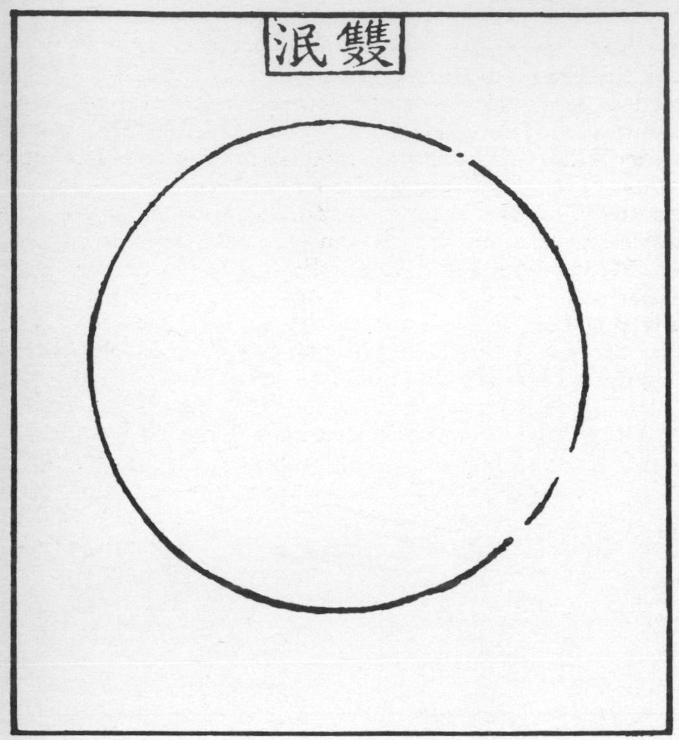

10. *Both Vanished*

Both the man and the animal have disappeared, no
traces are left,
The bright moon-light is empty and shadowless with
all the ten-thousand objects in it;
If anyone should ask the meaning of this,
Behold the lilies of the field and its fresh sweet-
scented verdure.

V. FROM THE JAPANESE ZEN MASTERS

Dai-o (1235–1308), Daito (1282–1336), and Kwanzan (1277–1360) are the three outstanding luminaries in the history of the Japanese Rinzai school of Zen. All the masters of this school now in Japan are their descendants. Dai-o went to China and studied Zen under Kido (Hsu-t'ang) in southern China, whose high expectations of the foreign disciple were fully justified as we can testify in the Japanese history of Zen. Daito is the founder of Daitokuji monastery and Kwanzan that of the Myoshinji, both of Kyoto. Muso (1273–1351) who followed another lineage of the Zen masters was versatile in artistic accomplishments. There are many noted gardens designed by him which are still well preserved. He was the founder of many Zen temples throughout Japan, among which the most notable one is Tenryuji at Saga, near Kyoto. Hakuin (1685–1768) is the father of modern Rinzai Zen. Without him it would be hard to tell the fate of Zen in Japan. He was no founder of a temple of any ecclesiastical importance; he lived his unpretentious life in a small temple in Suruga province, devoting himself to the bringing up of Zen monks and to the propagation of his teaching among laymen.

FROM THE JAPANESE ZEN MASTERS

I

Dai-o Kokushi "On Zen"

There is a reality even prior to heaven and earth;
Indeed, it has no form, much less a name;
Eyes fail to see it;
It has no voice for ears to detect;
To call it Mind or Buddha violates its nature,
For it then becomes like a visionary flower in the air;
It is not Mind, nor Buddha;
Absolutely quiet, and yet illuminating in a mysterious way,
It allows itself to be perceived only by the clear-eyed.
It is Dharma truly beyond form and sound;
It is Tao having nothing to do with words.

Wishing to entice the blind,
The Buddha has playfully let words escape his golden mouth;
Heaven and earth are ever since filled with entangling briars.

O my good worthy friends gathered here,
If you desire to listen to the thunderous voice of the Dharma,
Exhaust your words, empty your thoughts,
For then you may come to recognize this One Essence.
Says Hui the Brother, "The Buddha's Dharma
Is not to be given up to mere human sentiments."

2

Dai-o Kokushi's Admonition[1]

Those who enter the gate of Buddhism should first of all cherish a firm faith in the dignity and respectability of monkhood, for it is the path leading them away from poverty and humbleness. Its dignity is that of the sonship of the Dharmaraja of the triple world; no princely dignity which extends only over a limited area of the earth compares with it. Its respectability is that of the fatherhood of all sentient beings; no parental respectability belonging only to the head of a little family group equals it. When the monk finds himself in this position of dignity and respectability, living in the rock-cave of the Dharma where he enjoys the greatest happiness of a spiritual life, under the blissful protection of all the guardian gods of the Triple Treasure, is there any form of happiness that can surpass his?

The shaven head and the dyed garment are the noble symbols of Bodhisattvahood; the temple-buildings with all their ornamental fixtures are the honorific emblems of Buddhist virtue. They have nothing to do with mere decorative effects.

[1] Left to his disciples as his last words when he was about to pass away.

That the monk, now taking on himself these forms of dignity and respectability, is the recipient of all kinds of offerings from his followers; that he is quietly allowed to pursue his study of the Truth, not troubling himself with worldly labours and occupations—this is indeed due to the loving thoughts of Buddhas and Fathers. If the monk fails in this life to cross the stream of birth-and-death, when does he expect to requite all the kindly feelings bestowed upon him by his predecessors? We are ever liable as time goes on to miss opportunities; let the monk, therefore, be always on the watch not to pass his days idly.

The one path leading up to the highest peak is the mysterious orthodox line of transmission established by Buddhas and Fathers, and to walk along this road is the essence of appreciating what they have done for us. When the monk fails to discipline himself along this road, he thereby departs from the dignity and respectability of monkhood, laying himself down in the slums of poverty and misery. As I grow older I feel this to be my greatest regret, and, O monks, I have never been tired day and night of giving you strong admonitions on this point. Now, on the eve of my departure, my heart lingers with you, and my sincerest prayer is that you are never found lacking in the virtue of the monkish dignity and respectability, and that you ever be mindful of what properly belongs to monkhood. Pray, pray, be mindful of this, O monks!

This is the motherly advice of Nampo;[1] old monk-mendicant of Kencho Monastery.

3

Daito Kokushi's Admonition

O you, monks, who are in this mountain monastery, remember that you are gathered here for the sake of religion and not for the sake of clothes and food. As long as you have

[1] This is Dai-o Kokushi's own name, Dai-o being his posthumous honorary title.

shoulders [that is, the body], you will have clothes to wear, and as long as you have a mouth, you will have food to eat. Be ever mindful, throughout the twelve hours of the day, to apply yourselves to the study of the Unthinkable. Time passes like an arrow, never let your minds be disturbed by worldly cares. Ever, ever be on the look-out. After my departure, some of you may preside over five temples in prosperous conditions, with towers and halls and holy books all decorated in gold and silver, and devotees may noisily crowd into the grounds; some may pass hours in reading the sutras and reciting the dharanis, and sitting long in contemplation may not give themselves up to sleep; they may, eating once a day and observing the fastdays, and, throughout the six periods of the day, practise all the religious deeds. Even when they are thus devoted to the cause, if their thoughts are not really dwelling on the mysterious and untransmissible Way of the Buddhas and Fathers, they may yet come to ignore the law of moral causation, ending in a complete downfall of the true religion. All such belong to the family of evil spirits; however long my departure from the world may be, they are not to be called my descendants. Let, however, there be just one individual, who may be living in the wilderness in a hut thatched with one bundle of straw and passing his days by eating the roots of wild herbs cooked in a pot with broken legs; but if he single-mindedly applies himself to the study of his own [spiritual] affairs, he is the very one who has a daily interview with me and knows how to be grateful for his life. Who should ever despise such a one? O monks, be diligent, be diligent.[1]

Daito Kokushi's Last Poem

Buddhas and Fathers cut to pieces—
The sword is ever kept sharpened!
Where the wheel turns,
The void gnashes its teeth.

[1] In those monasteries which are connected in some way with the author of this admonition, it is read or rather chanted before a lecture or *Teisho* begins.

IV

Kwanzan Kokushi's Admonition[1]

It was in the Shogen period (1259) that our forefather the venerable Dai-o crossed the stormy waves of the great ocean in order to study Zen in Sung. He interviewed Hsu-t'ang (Kido) the great Zen master at Ching-tz'u (Jinzu) and under him Dai-o whole-heartedly devoted himself to the realization of Zen experience. Finally at Ching-shan (Kinzan) he was able to master all the secrets belonging to it. For this reason he was praised by his master as "having once more gone over the path", and the prophecy was also given him that his "descendants would ever be increasing". That the rightful lineage of the Yang-ch'i (Yogi) school was transported to this country of ours is to be ascribed to the merit of our venerable forefather.

Daito, my old venerable teacher, followed the steps of Dai-o who stayed in the western part of the capital; personally attending on him, he was in close contact with the master during his residence at Manju in Kyoto and at Kencho in Kamakura. Throughout the many years of attendance Daito never laid himself on a bed for sleep. He reminds us in many respects of the ancient worthies. When finally he mastered Zen, the venerable Dai-o gave him his testimony but ordered him to mature his experience for twenty years in quiet retirement. Surely enough, he proved to be a great successor truly worthy of his illustrious master, Dai-o. He resuscitated Zen which had been in a state of decline; he left an admonition for his followers to be ever mindful of keeping vigorously alive the true spirit of Zen discipline; all this is his merit.

[1] Muso Daishi is the honorific title posthumously given by an Emperor to Kwanzan Kokushi, the founder of Myoshinji, Kyoto, which is one of the most important Zen headquarters in Japan. All the Zen masters of the present day in Japan are his descendants. Some doubt is cherished about the genuineness of this Admonition as penned by Kwanzan himself, on the ground that the content is too "grandmotherly".

That in obedience to the august order of his Holiness the Ex-Emperor Hanazono I have come to establish this monastery, is due to the motherly love of my late master who chewed food for his helpless baby. O my followers, you may some day forget me, but if you should forget the loving thoughts of Dai-o and Daito, you are not my descendants. I pray you to strive to grasp the origin of things. Po-yun (Hakuun) was impressed with the great merit of Pai chang (Hyakjo), and Hu-ch'iu (Kokyu) was touched with the words of warning given by Po-yun (Hakuun). Such are our precedents. You will do well not to commit the fault of picking leaves or of searching for branches, [instead of taking hold of the root itself].

V

Muso Kokushi's Admonition

I have three kinds of disciples: those who, vigorously shaking off all entangling circumstances, and with singleness of thought apply themselves to the study of their own [spiritual] affairs, are of the first class. Those who are not so single-minded in the study, but scattering their attention are fond of book-learning, are of the second. Those who, covering their own spiritual brightness, are only occupied with the dribblings of the Buddhas and Fathers are called the lowest. As to those minds that are intoxicated by secular literature and engaged in establishing themselves as men of letters and are simply laymen with shaven heads, they do not belong even to the lowest. As regards those who think only of indulging in food and sleep and give themselves up to indolence—could such be called members of the Black Robe? They are truly, as were designated by an old master, clothes-racks and rice-bags. Inasmuch as they are not monks, they ought not to be permitted to call themselves my disciples and enter the monastery and sub-temples as well; even a temporary sojourn is to be prohibited, not to speak of their application as student-monks. When an old man like myself speaks thus, you may think he is lacking in all-embracing love, but the main thing is to let them know of their own faults, and, reforming themselves, to become growing plants in the patriarchal gardens.

VI

HAKUIN'S "SONG OF MEDITATION"

Sentient beings are primarily all Buddhas:
It is like ice and water,
Apart from water no ice can exist;
Outside sentient beings, where do we find the Buddhas?
Not knowing how near the Truth is,
People seek it far away,—what a pity!
They are like him who, in the midst of water,
Cries in thirst so imploringly;
They are like the son of a rich man
Who wandered away among the poor.
The reason why we transmigrate through the six worlds
Is because we are lost in the darkness of ignorance;
Going astray further and further in the darkness,
When are we able to get away from birth-and-death?

As regards the Meditation practised in the Mahayana,
We have no words to praise it fully:
The virtues of perfection such as charity, morality, etc.,
And the invocation of the Buddha's name, confession, and ascetic discipline,
And many other good deeds of merit,—
All these issue from the practice of Meditation;

Even those who have practised it just for one sitting
Will see all their evil karma wiped clean;
Nowhere will they find the evil paths,
But the Pure Land will be near at hand.
With a reverential heart, let them to this Truth
Listen even for once,
And let them praise it, and gladly embrace it,
And they will surely be blessed most infinitely.

For such as, reflecting within themselves,
Testify to the truth of Self-nature,
To the truth that Self-nature is no-nature,
They have really gone beyond the ken of sophistry.
For them opens the gate of the oneness of cause and effect,
And straight runs the path of non-duality and non-trinity.
Abiding with the not-particular which is in particulars,
Whether going or returning, they remain for ever unmoved;
Taking hold of the not-thought which lies in thoughts,
In every act of theirs they hear the voice of the truth.
How boundless the sky of Samadhi unfettered!
How transparent the perfect moon-light of the fourfold Wisdom!
At that moment what do they lack?
As the Truth eternally calm reveals itself to them,
This very earth is the Lotus Land of Purity,
And this body is the body of the Buddha.

VI. THE BUDDHIST STATUES AND PICTURES IN A ZEN MONASTERY

Visitors to a Zen monastery in Japan will be greeted by various Buddhist figures enshrined in the different parts of the institution. This section is devoted to the description of such figures.

I

The Buddha

Each Buddhist sect in Japan has its own *Honzon*, i.e. "the chief honoured one" as its main object of worship: for instance, the Jodo and the Shin have Amida Nyorai; the Shingon, Dainichi Nyorai (Mahavairocana); the Nichiren and the Zen, Shaka Nyorai (Sakyamuni). But this tradition is not uniformly observed by the Zen sect and much latitude has been allowed to the founder of each temple or monastery. The Buddha Sakyamuni is the proper one no doubt for all Zen institutions, for Zen claims to transmit the Buddha-heart—the first transmission taking place between Sakyamuni and Mahakashyapa. Sakyamuni thus occupies the main seat of honour on the Zen altar. But frequently we find there a statue of Kwannon (Avalokitesvara), or Yakushi (Bhaishajyaguru), or Jizo (Kshitigarbha), or Miroku (Maitreya), or even a trinity of Amida, Shaka, and Miroku. In this latter case Amida is the Buddha of the past, Shaka of the present, and Miroku of the future.

When the Honzon is Sakyamuni he is sometimes attended by a pair of Bodhisattvas and another of Arhats. The Bodhisattvas are Monju (Manjusri) and Fugen (Samantabhadra), and the Arhats are Kasho (Mahakashyapa) and Anan (Ananda). Sakyamuni is here both historical and "metaphysical", so to speak. Seeing him attended by his two chief disciples, he is a historical figure, but with Monju and Fugen who represent or symbolize wisdom and love, the two ruling attributes of the highest Reality, Sakyamuni is Vairocana standing above the world of transmigrations. Here we see the philosophy of the *Avatamsaka* or *Gandavyuha* incorporated into Zen. In fact, our religious life has two aspects—the experience itself and its philosophy.

This is represented in Buddhism by the historical trinity of Sakyamuni, Kashyapa, and Ananda, and by the metaphysical one of Vairocana, Manjusri, and Samantabhadra. Ananda stands for learning, intellection, and philosophizing; Kashyapa for life, experience, and realization; and Sakyamuni naturally for the unifying body in which experience and intellection find their field of harmonious co-operation. That religion needs philosophy is sometimes forgotten, and one of the great merits achieved by Buddhism is that it has never ignored this truth, and wherever it is propagated it helps the native genius of that land to develop its philosophy or to supply an intellectual background to its already-existing beliefs.

Perhaps it is only in the Zen monastery that the birth of the Buddha, his Enlightenment, and his Nirvana are commemorated. Mahayana Buddhism is much given up to the idealistic or metaphysical or transcendental interpretation of the historical facts so called in the life of the Buddha, and the evolution of the Bodhisattva-ideal has pushed the historical personages to the background. Vairocana or Amitabha has thus come to take the place of Sakyamuni Buddha, and a host of Bodhisattvas has completely displaced the Arhats.

But Zen has not forgotten the historical side of the Buddha's life. While Zen is not apparently concerned with earthly affairs, the fact that it has been nurtured in China, where history plays an important rôle in the cultural life of the people, points to its connection again with the earth. So the three most significant events in the development of Buddhism are properly remembered and elaborate rituals are annually performed at all the main Zen monasteries in Japan for the Buddha's birth-day, his attainment of Enlightenment, and his entrance into Nirvana.[1]

[1] Respectively: April 8, December 8, and February 15.

The Buddha's birth as represented by Zen followers places him in the most remarkable contrast to that of Christ. The baby Buddha is made to stand straight up with his right hand pointing at heaven and with his left at the earth, and he exclaims: "Above the heavens and below the heavens, I alone am the honoured one!" The voice reaches the furthest ends of the chiliocosm, and all the living beings—even matter is not dead in Buddhism—share in the joy of the Buddha's birth, realizing that they too are destined to be Buddhas.

On April 8 this baby Buddha standing in a bronze basin is taken out of the shrine, and the ceremony of baptizing the baby with sweet tea made of some vegetable leaves is performed; the tea thus used is afterwards given away to children. Recently, the celebration of this day takes place on a grand scale in all the larger cities of Japan, not only by Zen followers but by all Buddhists including monks, priests, laymen, laywomen, and children.

Sakyamuni as the Enlightened One sits on the lotus throne enshrined in the main hall of the Zen monastery. He is generally in the meditation posture.

The Nirvana scene is generally represented pictorially, except perhaps the one at the Nirvana Hall of Myoshinji, Kyoto, which is a bronze-slab. The most noted Nirvana picture is by Chodensu, of Tofukuji, the whole length of which is about sixteen yards.

Sakyamuni the Buddha in Meditation Posture

Buddha Attended by Two Bodhisattvas and Two Arhats

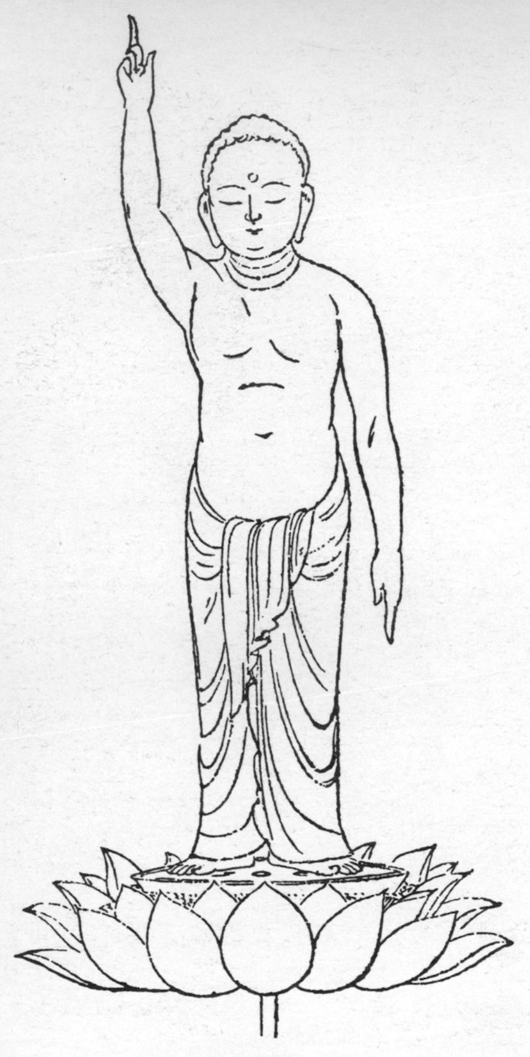

The Buddha's Birth

Buddha's Entrance into Nirvana

Bhaishajyaguru (Yakushi Nyorai)

II

The Bodhisattvas

When Sakyamuni is not found in the Main Buddha Hall, one of the following Bodhisattvas is enshrined in his place: Monju (Manjusri), Fugen (Samantabhadra), Kwannon (Avalokitesvara), Yakushi (Bhaishajyaguru), Miroku (Maitreya), Jizo (Kshitigarbha), or sometimes Kokuzo (Akasagarbha).

Monju and Fugen generally go in pairs and are the chief Bodhisattvas in the Avatamsaka (Kegon) conception of the world. Monju stands for Prajna. Sitting on a lion he holds a sword which is meant to cut all the intellectual and affectional entanglements in order to reveal the light of transcendental Prajna. Fugen is found on an elephant and represents love, Karuna. Karuna is contrasted with Prajna in that Prajna points to annihilation and to identity whereas Karuna points to construction and to multiplicity. The one is intellectual and the other emotional; the one unifies and the other diversifies. Fugen's ten vows are well known to students of the Kegon.

Kwannon is exclusively the Bodhisattva of compassion. In this respect he resembles Fugen. A special chapter is devoted to him in the *Hokkekyo* (*Saddharma-pundarika*) and also in the *Ryogonkyo* (*Suramgama*). He is one of the most popular Bosatsus or Bodhisattvas of Mahayana Buddhism. For an English translation of the *Kwannongyo* as rendered into Chinese by Kumarajiva see p. 30 of the present *Manual*.

Yakushi is the Bodhisattva-doctor. He holds a medicine jar in his hands and is attended by twelve gods each of whom represents one of his twelve vows. The main object of his appearance among us is to cure us of ignorance, which is the most fundamental of all the ills the flesh is heir to.

Jizo is principally or popularly the protector of children nowadays, but his original vows are to save us from wandering in the six paths of existence. He thus divides himself into six forms each of which stands as guardian in each one of the six paths. Hence the six Jizo we often find by the country roadside. He is generally represented in priestly robe, with a shaven head, and carries a long walking staff in his hand. In the Kamakura and the Ashikaga period he was quite a popular object of worship, and we find many fine artistic sculptures of this Bodhisattva in Kamakura.

Miroku is the future Buddha and at present has his abode in the Tushita Heaven waiting for his time to appear among us. He is also essentially compassionate as his name implies. He is sometimes called a Buddha and sometimes a Bodhisattva. Although he is supposed to be in one of the heavens, he is frequently encountered on earth.

Manjusri (Monju Bosatsu)

Samantabhadra (Fugen Bosatsu)

Avalokitesvara (Kwannon Bosatsu)

Maitreya (Miroku Bosatsu)

Kshitigarbha (Jizo Bosatsu)

III

The Arhats

The Arhats, generally sixteen in number, are enshrined in the second storey of the tower gate. They are all registered as dwellers in some remote mountains, and each is the leader of a large following. Their superficially grotesque and irregular appearances contrast in a strange way with those of the Bodhisattvas. They are miracle workers and tamers of the wild beasts. This characteristic seems to have excited the interest of the Zen monk-artist who has turned them into one of the favourite objects of his artistic imagination.

In a large Zen monastery the five hundred Arhats are given a special shelter in the premises.

Bhadrapala is one of the sixteen Arhats and had his *satori* while bathing. He is now enshrined in a niche in the bath-room attached to the Meditation Hall. When the monks take their bath, they pay respect to his figure.[1] The picture shown below belongs to Engakuji, Kamakura, and is one of the national treasures of Japan.

[1] *The Training of the Zen Monk*, p. 40.

Five of the Sixteen Arhats

Six of the Sixteen Arhats

Five of the Sixteen Arhats

IV

The Protecting Gods

Of the many protecting gods of Buddhism the following may be counted as belonging more or less exclusively to Zen, and they have each his or her own special quarter where they perform their several official duties for Buddhism.

The Niwo or "two guardian kings" are found enclosed at either side of the entrance gate. They represent the Vajra god in two forms; the one is masculine with the mouth tightly closed, and the other is feminine with an opened mouth. They guard the holy place from intruders.

The Shitenno or the four guardian gods are enshrined in the Buddha-hall at the four corners of the altar. Of these gods the most popular one is Tamonten (Vaisravana), the guardian of the North. This fact comes perhaps from his being the god of learning and also of wealth.

It is difficult to trace historically how Benzaiten (Sarasvati), who is the goddess of the River, finds her shrine in a Zen monastery. Some say that Benzaiten is not Sarasvati but Sridevi. Whoever she may be, a female form is often found among the audience of a saintly priest, and later she appears in his dream telling him how she who was formerly an enemy of Buddhism is now enlightened and will be one of its protectors, and so on. In any event there is room even in the Zen monastery, where the severest kind of asceticism is supposed to prevail, for a goddess to enter.

Idaten is a god of the kitchen looking after the provisions of the Brotherhood. The original Sanskrit term for it seems to be Skanda and not Veda as may be suggested from *i-da* or *wei-t'o*. He is one of the eight generals belonging to Virudhaka, the guardian god of the Southern quarter. He is a great runner and wherever there is a trouble he is instantly found there. In the Chinese monastery he occupies an important seat in the hall of the four guardian gods, but in the Japanese he is in the little shrine attached to the monks' dining-room.[1]

Ususama Myowo is a god of the lavatory. Ucchushma in Sanskrit means "to dry", "to parch", that is, to clean up filth by burning, by fire, for fire is a great purifying agency. Myowo is Vidyaraja, a special class of the gods who assume a form of wrath.[2]

Sambo Kojin seems to be a Japanese mountain god in the form of an Indian god. He is found outside the temple buildings. As the monasteries are generally located in the mountains this god who is supposed to preside over such districts, is invited to have his residence in the grounds so that he would be a good protector of the Brotherhood against the inimical influence of evil spirits.

Daikokuten whose Indian prototype is sometimes regarded as Mahakala is at present a purely Japanese god. He carries a large bag over his shoulder and stands on rice bales. Though his phallic origin is suspected, he has nothing, as he is, to do with it. He is a god of material wealth and like Idaten looks after the physical welfare of the Brotherhood. He is not such a universal object of respect in the Zen monastery.

Wherever the Prajnaparamita is preached or copied or recited, the sixteen "good gods" stand about the place and guard the devoted spirits against their being lured away by the enemy. As Zen is connected with the philosophy of Prajna they are also the gods of Zen. The picture below shows more than sixteen figures. Of the extra four personages standing in the foreground the two on the left are the Jotai Bosatsu (Sadaprarudita) and Jinsha Daio while the two on the right are Hsuan-Chuang with a kind of carrying-case on his back and Hoyu Bosatsu (Dharmodgata). Jotai and Hoyu are the principal characters in the *Prajnaparamita* as told in the second series of my *Essays in Zen Buddhism*. Hsuan-chuang is the translator of the *Mahaprajnaparamita Sutra* in six hundred fascicles and also that of Nagarjuna's commentary

[1] See also my *Training of the Zen Monk*, p. 106.
[2] Ibid., p. 44.

on the sutra in one hundred fascicles. While he was travelling through the desert, he was accosted by Jinsha, the god of the wilderness, who was responsible for the unsuccessful trips repeatedly attempted by the devoted Chinese pilgrims to India prior to Hsuan-chuang. The god was carrying six of the skulls of such victims about his neck. Listening to the *Prajnaparamita* as recited by Hsuan-chuang, he was converted and became a most devoted protector of the holy text. Hence his presence here.

The Two Door-Keeping Gods (Niwo)

The Four Guardian Gods

Benzaiten

Sambokojin

Skandadeva (Idaten)

Ucchushma (Ususamaten)

Mahakala (Daikokuten)

V

Some of the Historical Figures

Besides these mythical personages the Zen monastery gives shelter to some other historical characters deeply connected not only with Zen but with Buddhism as a whole. Bodhidharma as founder of Zen Buddhism naturally occupies a chief seat of honour beside the Buddha Sakyamuni. With Japanese Zen followers, however, the founder of a given temple is more highly honoured, and in each of the principal Zen institutions in Japan there is a special hall dedicated to the founder of that particular monastery, where an oil-lamp is kept burning all day and night. Bodhidharma is a unique figure and may be identified wherever he is. He is one of the favourite subjects for the Zen masters to try their amateurish brush. Kwannon is perhaps another such subject.

Fudaishi (Fu Ta-shih), also known as Zenne Daishi (Shan-hui), 493–564, was a contemporary of Bodhidharma. Although he does not belong to the orthodox lineage of Zen transmission, his life and sermons as recorded in the *Transmission of the Lamp* (*Ch'uan-teng Lu*)[1] are full of Zen flavour, so to speak. His famous gatha is well known to all Zen students.[2] Tradition makes him the inventor of what is known as Rinzo (*luntsang*), which is a system of revolving shelves for keeping the Chinese Tripitaka. For this reason he, together with his two sons, is set up in the Buddhist library as a kind of god of literature.

The Zen monastery harbours many old eccentric characters of whom the most noted of a Chinese origin are Kanzan (Han-shan) and Jittoku (Shih-te).[3] They are vagabond poet-ascetics. Another belonging to this group of

[1] Fas. XXVII.

[2] *Introduction to Zen Buddhism*, p. 58.

[3] *Zen Essays*, III, Plates XIV and XV, with their accompanying explanations.

characters is Hotei (Pu-tai).[1] That Hotei plays quite a different rôle in Japanese Buddhism from what he does in China I have explained in my article in the *Eastern Buddhist*, VI, 4, "Impressions of Chinese Buddhism".

Shotoku Taishi (574–622) was really one of the most remarkable figures in the cultural history of Japan, and it is no wonder that all the Japanese Buddhists pay special tribute to his memory by enshrining his statue in one of the monastery buildings. One of the legendary stories circulating in Japan with regard to Bodhidharma is that he came to Japan after he had finished his work in China and was found in the form of a miserable beggar at Kataoka Yama, near Nara. Shotoku Taishi met him there and it is said that they exchanged poems.

[1] *Ibid.* Plates X and XVI, and also Second Series.

Daruma (Ta-mo, Bodhidharma)

Shotoku Taishi

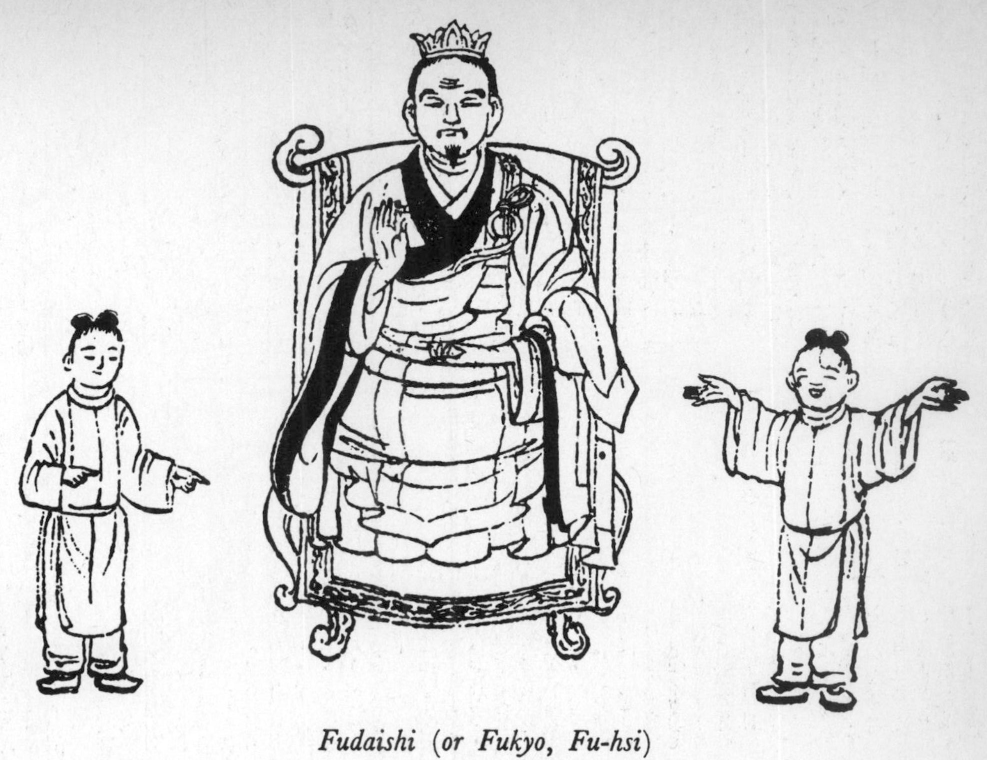

Fudaishi (or Fukyo, Fu-hsi)

INDEX

"ABRUPT" school (or teaching), 85, 86, 98, 100, 101
Absolute Reason, 81
Aggregates, five (*skandha*), 89
Akshayamati, 30 fn.
Alayavijnana, 51, 52, 53, 54
All-sided One, 38
Amanushya, 34, 35
Amida Nyorai (Amitabha), 17, 153, 154
Anagamin, 42
Ananda (Anan), 16, 65, 68, 153, 154
Anathapindada, 38
Aranasamadhi, 42
Arhatship, 42
Artha, 83
Aryavalokitesvara, 28
Asamskrita, 70, 94 fn., 95
Asura, 35, 44, 47
Asvaghosha, 51
Attachment, deep-seated, 62, 63
Avalokitasvara, 30 fn.
Avalokitesvara. See under *Kwannon*
Avatamsaka (Kegon), 154, 161
Avidya, 29
Ayatana, 53, 54, 55, 67
BASO (Ma-tsu), the great teacher, 104, 106, 107, 110, 111
Beings, four classes of, 35
"Believing in Mind", 76
Bell, 20; to strike the, 69
Benefaction, fourfold, 19
Benzaiten (Sarasvati), 172, 177
Bhadrapala, 168
Bhava, 29
Bhikshuni, 34
Bhikshus, 19, 28, 34, 38
Birth-and-death (*samsara*), 15, 50, 52, 87, 93, 94, 106, 108, 147
Blue-necked one, 22
Bodhi, 27, 76 fn., 84, 105, 117
Bodhidharma (Tamo, Daruma), 50, 104, 183, 184
Bodhisattva (Bosatsu), 27, 28, 30, 76 fn.; the life of the, 15, 32, 33, 34, 35
Bodhisattva-Mahasattvas, 18, 19
Bodhisattvasila Sutra, 87
Body-form (*rupakaya*), 40
Bosatsu. See *Bodhisattva*
Brahma, 33, 37
Brahman, 34
Buddha, 14, 16, 17 fn., 18, 19, 21, 27, 30, 32, 33, 76 fn., 111, 117, 145; and sentient beings, 112 fn.; attended by two Bodhisattvas, 157; body of the, 152; Mind is the, 113, 119; One Mind only is the, 113; Seven Buddhas, 15
Buddha-crown, 24
Buddha-essence, 117
Buddha-form, 33
Buddha-knowledge, 47
Buddha-land, 43, 62, 117
Buddha-mind, 109, 110, 117
Buddha-nature, 89, 95
Buddha's Birth, 158
Buddha-truth, 14
Buddhi, 62
CAKRAVARTIN, 33, 49, 55
Calamities or disasters, eight kinds of, 18, 19
Causation, or Causality, 74, 75, 96, 109, 148; Twelvefold Chain of (*pratityasamutpada*), 29
Chaitya, 47
Charity (*dana*), 39, 40, 41, 43, 76, 94, 98, 151
"Cheng-tao Ke", 89 fn.
Chieh, or *Chieh-t'o*, or *Chieh-sang*, 13
Ch'ih-kou, 126
Chodensu, 155
Chu-hung, 129
Citta, 49 fn., 54, 105
Cleansing the Karma-hindrances, Sutra on, 102 fn.
Compassion, 35, 37, 38, 57
Compassionate heart, 22, 36
Confession, 13, 151
DAIKOKUTEN (Mahakala), 173, 181
Dainichi Nyorai (Mahavairocana), 153

Dai-o Kokushi, 145, 146, 149, 150
Daito Kokushi, 145, 147, 149, 150
Defilement (or the defiled), 16, 22, 29, 75, 95, 131, 133
Denshin Hoyo, 112
Deva, 19, 35, 44, 47
Dharani, 17 fn., 18, 62; explained, 21
"Dharani of Removing Disasters", 21
"Dharani of the Victorious Buddha-Crown", 23
Dharanindhara, 38 fn.
Dharma, the, 13, 14, 16, 19, 29, 33, 34, 35, 40 fn., 41, 42, 43, 46, 60, 61, 79, 82, 87, 94, 98, 99, 116, 117, 118, 145, 146. See also *Teaching*
Dharma of Solitude (*vivikta-dharma*), 51
Dharma-banner, 98
Dharma-body, 89, 97
Dharmadhatu, 15, 16, 84
Dharma-drum, 97
Dharma-essence, 109
Dharma-food, 18
Dharma-hall, 122
Dharmakaya, 15, 55, 82
Dharma-king, 103, 108
Dharma-materials, 96
Dharma-megha, 55
Dharmaraja, 103, 108
Dharma-thunder, 97
Dhatu, 27, 29, 53, 54, 67
Dhyana, 76 fn., 93, 103, 105; four kinds of, 60
Dipankara Buddha, 43, 48, 94, 117
Discrimination, 51, 52, 58, 61, 63, 73, 96
Duhkha, 30
EASTERN *Buddist, The*, 183
Eckhart, 133 fn.
Egolessness (*anatman*), 56, 57, 61; twofold, 53
Ego-substance, 56, 61, 90
Emancipation (*moksha*), 39; eightfold, 92; the triple, 56
Emptiness (*sunyata*), 26, 29, 56, 67, 75, 76, 77, 78, 90, 96, 108, 117, 134 fn.; form is, 67
Samadhi of, 109; the threefold nature of, 76; twenty forms of, 99
Enlightenment, 15, 46, 79, 102, 119, 154, 155; deep, 28; final, 71; perfect, 91; supreme, 18, 20, 38, 39, 41, 47, 48, 49, 56, 57, 103
Entrance, the twofold, 73
"Entrance by Conduct", 73, 74
"Entrance by Reason", 73, 74
Essence, 79, 94, 99, 115
Evil paths, 24. See also under *Existence*
Excellence, thirty-two marks of, 55
Existence, five paths of, 24, 64; paths of, 18; six paths of, 90; three evil paths of, 18, 19
Eyes, the five, or the fivefold eyesight, 91, 119
FAMILIES, five, 97
Fearlessness (*nirbhaya*), 34, 93, 102
First Patriarch, 106. See also *Bodhidharma*
Five hundred Arhats, 168
Form (*rupa*), 28, 94; one sees by, 49, 50; the idea of, 39, 40
Fudaishi (Fu Ta-shih), 182, 186
Fugen (Samantabhadra), 115, 153, 154, 164
Function, sixfold, 91
GANDHARVA, 34, 58
Gandavyuha, 154
Ganga, the, 43
Ganga-sands, 18, 43, 45, 47, 93, 103, 115
Garbha, 51
Garuda, 34, 35
Gatha, 73; explained, 13
Gem, 119; a perfect, 96
Gensha (Hsuan-sha), 120, 122, 123
Goroku (*yu-lu*), 73
Goso (Wu-tsu), 124
Great Vehicle (Mahayana), 85

Great Way, 79
Greed, anger, and folly (the three poisons), 13, 55, 58, 64, 84
HABIT-ENERGY (*vasana*), 51, 58, 59, 60
Hakuin Zenji, 145, 151
Hannyakyo (*Prajnaparamita*), 26
Himalaya, 97
Hinayana Buddhism, 49 fn.
Hogen (Fa-yen), 123
Hokkekyo (*Saddharma-pundarika*), 30 fn., 50, 161
Hokoji (P'ang-yun), 110
Holy Path, 30 fn.
Honzon, 153
Hoshin, 17
Hotei (Pu-tai), 183
Hoyu Bosatsu (Dharmodgata), 173
Hsiang-wang, 126
Hsing-ssu, 105
Hsuan-chuang, 29
Huang-po (Wobaku Kiun), 112
Hu-ch'iu (Kokyu), 150
Hui-k'e, 50
Hui-neng, 73, 82, 89 fn., 104, 105, 106, 146
Hungry ghosts (*preta*), 16
ILA, or *Wei-t'o*, 172
Idaten (Skandadeva), 172, 179
Ignorance (*avidya*), 27, 78, 89
Impermanence, the Gatha of, 15
Indriya, 29; the six senses, 29
Interfusion, 20, 20 fn., 69; perfect, 70
Introduction to Zen Buddhism, An, 182 fn.
Invalids, three kinds of, 120
Iron Mountains, 20
Isvara, 33
JAMBUDIPA, 85
Jaramarana, 30
Jati, 29
Jeta, 38
Jiji Bosatsu, 38
Jinsha Daio, 173, 174
Jitoku Ki (Tzu-te Hui), 128, 129
Jittoku (Shih-te), 182
Jizo (Ti-tsang, Kshitigarbha), 123, 153, 161, 167; six, 162
Jnana, 88 fn.; fourfold, 92
Jodo, 153
Jotai Bosatsu (Sadaprarudita), 173
KAKU-AN Shi-on (Kuoan Shih-yuan), 127, 128, 129
Kalinga, 46
Kanroo, 17
Kanzan (Han-shan), 182
Karma, 13, 30, 47, 48, 67, 71, 74, 75, 90, 97, 99, 109, 117, 152
Karma-hindrances, 101
Karuna, 161
Kasho (Mahakashyapa), 98, 153, 154
Kido (Hsu-t'ang), 145, 149
Kinnara, 34, 35
Klesa, 89, 105
Koan, 120
Kohashin, 17
Kokuzo (Akasagarbha), 161
Kongokyo or *Diamond Sutra*, 38, 48 fn. See also *Vajracchedika*
Kongosammaikyo (*Vajrasamadhi*), 26
Kshanti, 46, 94
Ku tsun-hsiu yu-lu, 107 fn.
Kumarajiva, 30 fn., 38 fn., 65, 161
Kwanjizai, 30 fn., 101
Kwannon Bosatsu, or Kwanzeon Bosatsu (Avalokitesvara), 16, 20 fn., 22, 23, 26, 30, 30 fn., 31, 32, 36, 37, 38, 69, 121, 153, 161, 165, 182
Kwannongyo (*Samantamukha-parivarta*), 20 fn., 26, 30 fn., 70, 71, 161
Kwanzan Kokushi, 145, 149, 149 fn.
"*Kwatz!*", 121
LANKAVATARA Sutra (*Ryogakyo*), 26, 50, 51
Li-lou, 124, 126, 127
MAHA, 82, 83
Mahakashyapa. See *Kasho*
Mahamati, 50
Mahaprajna, 98
Mahaprajnaparamita, 18, 82

Mahayana, 26, 29, 38 fn., 47, 49 fn., 50, 65, 88, 151, 154
Mahayana sutras, 70
Mahesvara, 33
Mahoraga, 34, 35
Manas, 54, 105
Mani-gem, or Mani-jewel, 91, 95, 103
Manjusri. See *Monju*
Manovijnana, 40 fn., 54
Mantram, 27; called "Sitatara-patala", 65
Manushya, 34, 35
Marga, 30
Masters and Disciples of the Lanka, the, 76 fn., 80 fn.
Matanga, 65
Maya, 55, 63, 70
Meditation, 151
Memory (*vasana*), 51, 58
Merit, root of, 40
Mind (or absolute mind), 16, 29, 51, 52, 54, 57, 58, 59, 65, 75, 76 fn., 78, 80, 82, 83, 88, 96, 105, 109; One, 112, 113, 114, 115, 116; Original, 66, 87
Mind-attachment, 114
Mind-essence, 65, 66, 67, 68, 69, 70, 72, 105
Mind-only (*cittamatra*), 50, 51, 58
Miroku (Maitreya), 153, 161, 162, 166
Mondo, 105
Monju (Manjusri), 65, 66, 115, 153, 154, 161, 163
Mount Sumeru, 36, 43
Mujinni Bosatsu, 30, 31, 32, 33, 34, 35
Multitudinousness of external objects, 58
Muso Daishi, 149 fn.
Muso Kokushi, 145, 149 fn., 150
Myoshishin, 17
Myowo (Vidyaraja), 173
NAGA, 19, 34, 35, 36, 100
Nagarjuna, 173
Namarupa, 29
Nan-yueh Huai-jang, 105, 106
Nichiren, 30 fn., 153
Nirodha, 30
Nirvana, 16, 27, 39, 50, 52, 56, 70, 71, 76 fn., 91, 94 fn., 106, 154, 155, 159
Niwo, 172, 175
No-birth, 59, 94, 96, 102
Noble Truth, Fourfold, 30
Noble Wisdom (*arayajnana*), 51, 53, 57, 61
No-body, 43
No-dharma, 41
Non-discrimination, 56
Non-doing (*asamskara*), 41
Non-resistance, 43
OMITO, 17
One Essence, 108
One Nature, 97
Original Body, 110
Original Nature, 85, 86, 109
Original Vows (*pranidhana*), 57, 161
PAI-CHANG (Hyakjo), 111, 150
Pai-hsiu, 112
P'ang, 110
Paramita, 83; six, 24, 90; the first, 45
Paramiti (?), 65
Paravrittasraya, 52
Passions, evil, 37, 69, 108; three, 84, 85, 86
Path (Tao), 73
Paths, the six, 90, 161. See also under *Existence*
Perfect Way, 76
Perfection, six virtues of, 113
Pi-kuan, "wall-gazing", 74
Pi-yen Chi, 120 fn.
Poisons, the three, 89. See also *Greed, etc.*
Power, the fivefold, 91
Po-yun (Hakuun), 150
Prajna, 29, 38 fn., 69, 71, 76 fn., 83, 88 fn., 93, 96, 101, 103, 161, 173
Prajnaparamita, 26, 27, 28, 44, 48 fn., 76, 84, 86, 173
Prajnaparamita-hridaya Sutra, or *Hannya Shin-Gyo*, 26
Prajna-samadhi, 84

Prajna-wisdom, 85
Pratyaya, 113 fn.
Pratyekabuddha, 33, 61, 62
Pravesha, six, 67
Prayer, 16, 19, 20
Pu-ming, 129
Pure Land, or Land of Purity, 18, 106, 152
Purity, vows of, 35
RAFT, 41
Rahula, 69
Rajagriha, 28
Rakshasas, 31, 36
Reality, 80 fn., 89, 90, 95, 97, 154
Reality-limit (*bhutakoti*), 24, 56
Revulsion (*paravrittasraya*), 52
Riddhi, the six, 92 fn.
Rifui, 17
Rinzo (*lun-tsang*), 182
Ryogonkyo (*Suramgama*), 19, 20 fn., 26, 71, 64, 161
SADAYATANA, 29
Sagaramudra-samadhi, 108
Saha world, or *sahaloka*, 32, 34, 35,
Sakrendra, 33, 115
Sakridagamin, 42
Sakyamuni, Kashyapa, and Ananda, historical trinity of, 154, 157
Samadhi, 28, 108, 152
Samantabhadra. See *Fugen*
Samantamukha Parivarta, 30 fn.
Samatha, 69, 72
Sambo Kojin, 173, 178
Samjna, 28
Samskara, 28, 29
Samskrita, 50, 63, 70, 94, 94 fn.
Samudaya, 30
Sangha, 14, 16
Sariputra, 26, 28
Sarira, 14
Satori, 168
Seccho, 120 fn., 124, 125, 126
Seikyo (Ching-chu), 128, 129
Sekito (Shih-t'ou), 104, 106, 107
Self, 66
Self-nature, 24, 51, 84, 87, 152
Self-realization, 52, 57, 61
Self-substance, 58
Seng-t'san (Sosan), 76 fn.
Shaka Nyorai (Sakyamuni), 14, 16, 35, 94, 153, 154, 155, 156, 161, 182
Shen-hsiu, 104
Shih-k'uang, 125, 126
Shin, 153
Shingon, 30 fn., 65, 153
Shingyo (*Prajnaparamitahriddya*), 26
Shitenno, the Four Guardian Gods, 172, 176
Shotoku Taishi, 183, 185
Shubun, 129
Six paths, the, 90, 161, 162. See also *Existence*
Sixteen Arhats, 168, 169–71
Sixteen Good Gods of the Prajnaparamita (Hannya Juroku Zenji), 173; picture, facing 182
Skandha, 28, 54, 55, 67
Skilful means (*upayakausalya*), 33, 56
Sokei, 93, 98
Solitude, 64
"Song of Enlightenment", 89
Sparsa, 29
Sravaka, 33, 61, 107, 108, 109, 110
Sravakahood, 62
Sravasti, 38
Sreshthayana, 47
Sridevi, 172
Srotapanna, 42
Srotapannahood, 71
Stages, the ten, 19, 116
Statements, the five, 119
Sthamaprapta, 115
Subhuti, 39, 40, 41
Suchness (*tathata*), 24, 50, 67, 80, 81, 84, 87, 88, 115
Sugata, 24
Sunyata, 29, 70
Svabhava, the three, 54
TAHO, 17
Tahobutsu (Prabhutaratna Buddha), 35
Tamonten (Vaisravana), 172
Tan-ching, 82, 89 fn.

Tao, 73, 107, 108
Tao-wu (Dogo), 106
Tathagata, 13, 17, 24, 25; defined, 49; of Infinite Light, 17 fn., 18 fn.
Tathagata-dhyana, 90
Tathagata-garbha, 51, 55, 56, 67, 68, 69, 91
Tathagatahood, 57, 61, 95, 99
Tathagata-wheel, 99
Tathata, 61, 62
Teaching, of the Buddha, 15, 21, 41, 49, 97, 99; of the Tathagatas, 53, 102. See also *Dharma*
Teisho, 148 fn.
Ten Oxherding Pictures, the, 127
Tendai, 30 fn.
Thirty-two marks, 49; of a great man, 44, 45
Training of the Zen Buddhist Monk, 173 fn.
Transformation Body (*nirmana-kaya*), 62
Transmigration (*samsara*), 18, 54, 116
Transmission of the Lamp, The, 76 fn., 182
Treasures, seven precious, 41, 43
Triple Treasure (*triratna*), 18, 22, 23
Triple Vehicle (*triyana*), 116
Triple world (*triloka*), 18, 19, 23
Trishna, 29
Tsung-ch'ih, or *Neng-ch'ih*, 21
Tushita Heaven, the, 162
UMMON (Yun-men), 121, 123
Unborn, 53, 56, 93
Unthinkable, the, 93, 148
Upadana, 29
Upali, 102
Upasaka, 34
Upasika, 34
Ususama Myowo (Ucchushma), 173, 180
VAIROCANA, 154
Vaisravana, 33
Vajra, 24; god, 172; mountain, 36
Vajra-blade, 96
Vajracchedika, or *Vajracchedika-prajnaparamita Sutra*, 26, 38 fn., 50, 84, 85
Vajragarbha, 24
Vajrapani, 34
Vajra-prajna-paramita, 44
Vedana, 28, 29
Vehicles (*yana*), Major and Minor, 86; three, 97; two, 101
Vetala, 54
Vijnana, 28, 29, 51, 53, 54, 105; the six, 29, 70
Vimalakirti, 50, 102, 115
Vimoksha, the eight, 92 fn.
Vipasyana, 69, 70, 72
Virudhaka, 172
Vishaya, 54, 83; the six qualities, 29
Vows, Four Great, 14; inexhaustible, 62; universal, 35
WAY, 80; untransmissible, 148
Wisdom, fourfold, 152
Wu-hsin, or *mu-shin*, 114 fn., 116, 117, 118
YAJNADATTA, 68
Yakshas, 31, 34, 35
Yakushi (Bhaishajyaguru), 153, 160, 161
Yang-ch'i (Yogi), 149
Yathabhuta, 61
Yemmei, 16 fn.
Yemmei Kwannon, 16
Yengakukyo, 26
Yengo, 125, 127
Yoka Daishi, 89
Yuan, 113 fn.
Yuimakyo (*Vimalakirti-sutra*), 26, 87
Yu-lu (*goroku*), 73
Yuse (Yung-shih), 102
ZEN, 13, 26, 30 fn., 50, 94, 96, 102, 104, 107, 118, 122, 145, 153
Zen literature, 73
Zen monastery, 20 fn.
Zenne Daishi (Shan-hui). 182
Zensho (Shan-hsing), 100